FROM THE INTRODU...

ZIG ZIGL...

Author/Motivational Teacher

This book will enable parents and grandparents [to have]. . .special insights and wisdom as to the best way to communicate with their kids. [It will] draw families closer together. Good stuff—really good.

This book is beautifully written, profound in its wisdom. . .and humorous in a special way.

Because of the profound observations that are made through these kids, families will have even better relationships and will understand more about the God who loves and created us.

WHAT KIDS SAY ABOUT LIFE, LOVE, AND GOD

WHAT KIDS

SAY ABOUT LIFE, LOVE, AND GOD

MORE THAN 500 WITTY AND WISE INSIGHTS
THROUGH THE EYES OF A CHILD

Compiled by
MARY AND BILL BARBOUR
WITH REBEKAH RENDALL BLANDA

PROMISE
PRESS

Published by Promise Press, an imprint of Barbour Publishing, Inc., P.O. Box 719, Uhrichsville, Ohio 44683, http://www.promisepress.com

Member of the
Evangelical Christian
Publishers Association

DEDICATION

*You have been set apart as holy to the LORD your God,
and he has chosen you to be his own special treasure
from all the nations of the earth.*
DEUTERONOMY 14:2

This book is dedicated to children the world over,
especially to those boys and girls whose innermost thoughts and feelings
are expressed in this harvest of wisdom and wit.

CONTENTS

FOREWORD

We believe children have a lot to say to the grown-ups of this world, and so we have gathered the thoughts from the hearts and minds of children between the ages of two and ten. Families from everywhere supplied us with enough kids' quotes, experiences, and comments to fill a half-dozen books!

Compiling this book has been an especially meaningful experience for us because we have been privileged to glimpse the world from a child's perspective. These touching words about God, Jesus, and heaven are reminders that the Lord's kingdom belongs to those who love and trust Him fully. Children's thoughts about God, parents, grandparents, siblings, and home life have called to mind our own childhood and the influence our families had on us.

We hope you will be uplifted and encouraged by the wisdom and wit presented here. Perhaps you will think about God in a new way and realize anew the importance of family. And you'll probably have a good laugh! We pray that, like us, you will come to a fresh awareness that kids do matter and that adults must listen to them.

MARY AND BILL BARBOUR
REBEKAH RENDALL BLANDA

ACKNOWLEDGMENTS

Our heartfelt thanks to the parents, grandparents, and others who provided the children's thoughts, expressions, and stories that fill this book. Included among these contributors are missionaries associated with the Christian and Missionary Alliance, the Evangelical Lutheran Church in America, Operation Mobilization, OMS International, T.E.A.M., the United World Mission, and Wycliffe Bible Translators.

The able staff of Shirley Francess Secretariat in Fort Myers, Florida, was tireless in handling the technical aspects of the preparation of this manuscript. And *thank you!* to John Blanda for his ever-present and enthusiastic encouragement.

Thanks in heaping measure to all those who shared a special interest in this book project, including: Nell Baldwin, Jack Kreismer, Joan and Bill Brown, E. E. Owen, Betty and Eugene Dotter, Alice and Lyle Petersen, Pat Dys, Elisabeth Pissard, Ruth and Harold Greenlee, Lyla and George Sander, Elizabeth and Brad Hopkins, Kay and Bob Shade, Beulah and Dick Johnston, Jill Shaffer, Teresa Wiggins, and Rochelle Anderson.

INTRODUCTION

What Kids Say About Life, Love, and God is a "sleeper" that will be fully awake as soon as a few readers have dug into this book. It's beautifully written, profound in its wisdom and insight, encouraging in its approach, and downright funny and humorous in a special way. Years ago, Art Linkletter said, "Kids say the darndest things!" The authors demonstrate that kids say humorous, wise, and profound things along the way.

There is so much I could say about this book that the introduction would be longer than the book, but I am convinced that here is a book that will draw families closer together. If parents and grandparents will read this book to their children and grandchildren, they will be laughing—and, on occasion, crying—together. Because of the profound observations that are made through these kids, families will have even better relationships and will understand more about the God who loves and created us.

Not only will the book enable parents and grandparents to draw closer to their children and grandchildren, but it will also give them special insights and wisdom as to the best way to communicate with their kids. We need to always remember that kids are our hope for the future, but we are their hope for the present and the future. This book will help all of us relate better not only to our immediate families but also to other people. We will learn how to see life through the eyes of others, how to experience some of their joys, temptations, trials, and reversals, and become better people as a result.

One thing that strikes me is that we people do have something that

God doesn't have, and that's grandchildren. However, knowing how important they were and how much they would be loved, because God loves us, He gives us grandchildren. As I've often said, had my wife and I known that grandchildren were going to be so much fun, we certainly would have been nicer to their parents!

Our faith is in what Christ said in Matthew 11:25: "I praise you, Father, Lord of heaven and earth, because you have hidden these things from the wise and learned, and revealed them to little children" (NIV). As you read this book, you will discover the total truth of those words. Good stuff—really good.

ZIG ZIGLAR
Author/Motivational Teacher

Grandchildren are the
crowning glory of the aged;
parents are the pride of their children.

PROVERBS 17:6

How happy is the man whose quiver is full of them!
He will not be put to shame when he confronts
his accusers at the city gates.

PSALM 127:5

May you live to enjoy your grandchildren.

PSALM 128:6

1

Grandparents

X O X

*Yep, there's something wonderful about
my grandma and grandpa.*

NANCY, 7

Just when mysterious new aches and pains arise in your body, and time begins to pass much too rapidly, you learn of an approaching blessed event. Soon you hold the future in your arms—a newborn child! Life is sweet again. It is a grandparent's privilege to enjoy pretty babies, energetic toddlers, and affectionate youngsters with neither the responsibility nor the pressure of parenthood.

Children know there is something very special about their grandparents—a loving grown-up who knows their home, their parents, their siblings; who has plenty of time for reading books and playing games; with whom they have the freedom to do things that may not be allowed in their own home. Grandparents know when to say "yes"!

The relationship between a grandparent and a grandchild is unlike any other. For the child, a grandparent is a nonthreatening, secure, loving friend. And the grandparents benefit from knowing they are valued and needed.

Grandparents are in a unique position to impact their grandchildren's spiritual lives as well. For example, 2 Timothy 1:5 tells of Lois, who helped mold her grandson, the apostle Timothy, into a godly man. God has given grandparents a responsibility toward the young members of their family with the blessing and reward of guiding them as they grow and mature.

Truly, grandparents understand the truth in the saying, "Had I known grandchildren were so much fun, I would have had them first!"

Our six-year-old son, Christopher, was distraught over something and said, "I'm going to move away from here, and also I'm taking Grandpa with me; but we're not going very far."

X O X

My daughter, two-year-old Ashley, was learning the names of all her aunties. When we asked her to name them, she said, "Auntie Julie, Auntie Jeannie, Auntie Hope, and Auntie Grandma!"   AUSTRALIA

X O X

Just out of the hospital, my husband received this greeting: "Grandpa, I am so glad you didn't go up with your angels."

X O X

I just love to go toy shopping with my grandpa. Boy, does he ever buy me stuff!   GINNIE, 5

X O X

Sue told me a lot of grandfathers are grouchy. Not my two.   LINDA, 5

Our granddaughter was helping her grandfather water his garden. He said, "Do you know whose garden this is, Stephanie?" She replied, "It's Gram's garden." Later, when they were watering the flowers, he asked again, "Do you know whose roses these are, Stephanie?" She answered again, "They are Gram's roses." Still later, as they were working around the wishing well, he asked, "Do you know whose wishing well this is?" Once again, she answered, "It's Gram's wishing well." Her Grandfather said, "Well, if Gram has the garden, the roses, and the wishing well, then what does Pap have?" She looked up and smiled her three-year-old smile. "You got Gram."

✗ ○ ✗

Our grandson, age three, went through his ear of corn like a buzz saw. When finished, he observed his mom was just starting hers and asked, "Mom, wanna switch?"

✗ ○ ✗

Jennifer, six, and Laura, seven, were writing about what they wanted to be when they grow up. "A grandma," said Laura. "OK. But what would you write about being a grandma?" "Oh," said Laura, "that's 'cinchy.' You just go to the store, go to the doctor's office, and then go to the beauty shop to get your hair permed. That's all."

Prekindergartner Cole could hardly wait for his grandmother to drop off his mother at her office. As he watched his mother walk away, and they drove off, Cole said, "Okay, Gramma, now let's talk about bugs."

✗ O ✗

Grandma, when were you a baby?" asked our kindergartner Steven. I said, "Seventy years ago." He exclaimed, "Wow, that's a long time. No wonder you're wearing out."

✗ O ✗

Following the sudden death of their grandfather, Amanda, four, and Robbie, six, had to be informed of their loss. Their mother and grandmother quietly told the children of the passing of their beloved grandfather. Robbie choked up with tears, but Amanda, after a period of silence and deep thought, responded with, "If Grandmom gets married again, can I be the flower girl?"

✗ O ✗

One day our three-year-old granddaughter was unusually noisy. I said, "Jessica, why are you being so loud?" Without hesitating, she replied, "God made me this way, Nana!"

My grandparents are my special friends. Yep, there's something wonderful about my grandma and grandpa.

NANCY, 7

✗ ο ✗

Granny passed away when Kevin was about eight years old. On the day of the funeral, Kevin's auntie Nell arrived at school to pick him up for the funeral. When Nell arrived at school, Kevin said, "Oh, Auntie Nell, I knew someone would come to get me. I've been praying all morning."

✗ ο ✗

Our challenge on this particular weekend was to baby-sit our four-year-old grandson, Adam, while his parents attended a church conference. When we asked Adam about the "rules" of the house, he answered, "I'll tell you the rules: no milk at bedtime, no tobacco, alcohol, or drugs."

✗ ο ✗

My grandma is German. She knows the German words for lots of English words, but she don't know the English word for no. That's good!

BRETT, 8 (GERMANY)

It was a special morning at our church, and I was seated at the organ bringing the service to a conclusion, when I looked down the aisle and noticed the mother of three children in our church coming toward me.

When she got to the organ, she handed me a little photograph of their youngest child, Sarah. On the back of the photo was written: "With Love to Grandma Betty." That's the first time I knew I had a granddaughter! There was also a photo for my new-grandpa husband, with the words: "With Love to Grandpa Gene."

This was the beginning of a decades-long, loving relationship between my husband and me and this young family. Gene and I have kept in close touch with these folks and their three children—Greg, Justin, and Sarah. With the passing years, we were there for them and they for us. We saw each other occasionally, especially during the holiday seasons and other times special to them. Concerned we'd be by ourselves, they invited us for Thanksgiving dinners. Yes, for all intents and purposes, we were family.

The children came regularly to Sunday school and to church. Their mother taught them carefully at home, as well. On one special day, Greg, then five, and his mother had a little talk, and Greg accepted the Lord as his Savior. His mother thought it would be appropriate for him to tell Grandma Betty what he had just done. He did that nicely. I congratulated him, told him how happy I was for him, how proud of him I was—all of the grandmotherly things. And with joy and blessing at each end of the line, our conversation ended.

After just a few minutes, the phone rang; it was Greg's mother again —this time in tears. "Oh, Grandma Betty, I've done something all wrong. I've gotten Greg all mixed up. I don't know how I did it, but he's all mixed up." So I tried to calm her down and then said, "Now, tell me exactly what happened." She said, "Well, after he finished talking to you, Greg came and sat beside me on the couch. I hugged him and said, 'Oh, Greg, you're born again.' And he flung himself back on the couch, threw his hands up over his head, and said, 'Oh, no, diapers again!' "

This dear woman thought Greg had missed the whole point! The Lord helped me to remind her about the third chapter of John when Jesus told Nicodemus, a famous ruler of the Jews, that he needed to be born again. He said, "Do I have to enter my mother's womb and be born over again?" So I said, "If Nicodemus was confused, why not Greg?" This helped her—and soon it helped Greg to better understand the nature of the born-again experience.

Greg has grown up to be a fine young man—born again and no longer confused!

BETTY DOTTER (FORT MYERS, FLORIDA)

✗ O ✗

We were determined to have our twelve-year-old grandson see everything at Walt Disney World. After three full, hectic days, his comment: "Grandpa, we should've stayed home and just gone riding around in your golf cart. That's more fun than that Disney race!"

Our former pastor's mother was baby-sitting her two little grandsons. When she was ready to go home, Nathan, age six, asked, "Grandma, aren't you afraid to drive home in the dark?" Grandmother replied, "No, honey, I'm not afraid, because Jesus sits right here beside me in the car." One day, when Grandmother was going to take Nathan home with her, he said, "Grandma, do you think Jesus would mind sitting in the backseat, so I could sit here beside you?"

✗ O ✗

At dinner with our daughter and her family one evening—lots of fun and laughter—our six-year-old grandson said, "Grandpa, I wish you and Gram would hurry up and get old, so you could come and live with us."

✗ O ✗

During a Sunday school discussion about how we could all serve the church, Kyle, seven, grandson of our pastor, said, "Oh, not me. . .'cause my grandpa owns this church!"

✗ O ✗

My husband was slowly growing bald, but to keep up with the times had let his hair grow slightly longer in the back. One day while out with the grandchildren, Robbie said, "Grandpop, look at your hair. It's all slidden back!"

Visiting our eight-year-old grandson recently, I suggested a fishing trip. *This will be a special time together*, I thought. But he took me down a notch or two when he said, "Sorry, Gramps. Can't do. I have to be at my Web site then."

XOX

Three-year-old Kevin loved bugs, worms, and other wiggly things. He took a worm into Granny's house, and she made him take it back outside. He sat down on the steps outside and gave the worm a long talk about Granny; that although she did not love worms, he still loved Granny.

XOX

When Jason was about three, we explained to him about families—who was the mother and father, and so on. But when I said, "Grandma and Grandpa are my mother and father," he replied, "Aw, come on, Mom, you're fooling me!"

XOX

In Sunday school today, I learned the Bible says that Jesus knows all about everything and "even the very hairs on your head are numbered." Grandpa's bald—no problem there. But there aren't enough numbers in the whole world to count Grandma's hairs—one by one! HUGH, 9

I was ironing and sprinkling the clothes with water in the process. Laura, five, was observing this and asked me to explain. I said, "When you sprinkle and iron, it takes the wrinkles out." She then asked, "Do you think I could do that to Grandma's face?"

✗ O ✗

Young Jeremy was following Grandpa's every move, having a delightful time. In the afternoon, he came in and sat on the floor by me and very seriously said, "You know, I like Grandpa the very best. He is my favorite of everyone, even my other grandpa. He is the most fun and does lots of things with me—and, Grandma, you're a good cook!"   CANADA

✗ O ✗

Leaving after a week-long visit, I gave my granddaughter, three, a big hug and said, "I'll miss you so much and be lonesome for you." She replied, "You'll never be lonesome, Grandma; God is always with you."

✗ O ✗

One time we were going to fix ice cream cones for our young grandsons, but the ice cream, fresh from the freezer, was so hard we said we'd put it in the microwave. Alarmed, our four-year-old grandson said, "But, wait a minute. I like my ice cream cold!"

Sometimes my grandma surprises me. Even at her age, she knows hula hoops with water in them go around better than the kind she had when she was a girl.

GAIL, 6

✗ ○ ✗

It's a funny thing, my dad and my grandpa do stuff just alike—planting tulips, same way. Polishing brown shoes, same way. Talking to God before dinner, same words. My mom says, "Well, it figures, doesn't it?" I guess.

LARRY, 8

✗ ○ ✗

I just learned my grandma wears a wig. Know how I found out? She took us to a sort of like zoo where you pet the baby lambs, and they have other things running all over the place. Then this little monkey jumped on Nana's shoulder and pulled off her hair! Then we went home quickly.

MARK, 6 (WEST AFRICA)

✗ ○ ✗

Grandpas always eat slow and drive slow. And when they walk the dog— same thing. I suppose it's because they are over one hundred. When I asked Gramps about this, he answered, "Well now, let me just think about that question for a while."

IAN, 6

My grandma's really the smart one. When we go to a restaurant, she first asks, "Where's the rest room?" She knows that next to cheeseburgers, I like the bathroom best.　　　　　　　　　　　　　　　　　　SYLVIA, 5

✗ ○ ✗

Grandma to Abigail (three): "I'm going to miss you soooooo much when you leave. Will you miss me?" Abigail: "But I don't know how to miss you."

✗ ○ ✗

Little DeAndra had two grandfathers: the "brown-headed grandpa" and the "white-headed grandpa."

✗ ○ ✗

It's always "Punkin," "Big Guy," "Sonny," "Buddy"—like that. Will grandparents ever learn our right names?　　　　　　　　　　　　GLEN, 8

✗ ○ ✗

My granddaughter was three years old when she looked intently at me and said, "Grandma, how come you're older than Grandpa?" Taken off guard, I asked, "What made you ask that?" She replied, "Because you have so many wrinkles, and Grandpa has none!"

Grandpa was giving considerable loving attention to Ryan's newborn brother. Ryan told his mom, "I'm being silly, but I need somebody. I need my grandpa back!"

XOX

While talking about sin, my husband asked our young son Ethan, "Who was the one person who never sinned?" Ethan quickly answered, "Grandad."

XOX

When our ten-year-old granddaughter, Stephanie, came for a weekend, I prepared our family's favorite dish—chili. When asked if she liked chili, she said, "Yes, everything except the sauce and the beans." So I saved the chili for another day.

XOX

A neighbor gave our grandson Adam, age six, a book with blank pages that came alive with pictures when rubbed with a special pencil. I said, "I'd love to have had a book like that when I was little." Adam replied, "C'mon, Grandma, when you were a girl, they didn't even have pencils!"

"And I will be your Father,
and you will be
my sons and daughters,"
says the Lord Almighty.

2 CORINTHIANS 6:18

2

Family Life

X O X

Kids do brighten the corner where they live.

Families are the greatest influence on a young child. Mothers, fathers, sisters, and brothers all shape and direct a child's growth. In families, children learn how to get along, share, take responsibility, and care for others. In family life, children are truly accepted and loved, nurtured and trained. There they quickly learn that actions have consequences, as parents lovingly discipline and guide their young ones in God's way. As Ephesians 6:4 says, parents are to bring up their children "in the training and instruction of the Lord" (NIV).

Part of this training is how to get along with others—especially one's siblings. Be kind to one another, love one another, and think of others more highly than yourself. Even though sibling relationships are difficult at times, there is a strong and deep bond between these family members. The Bible shows Jacob and Esau reunited (Genesis 33), Joseph forgiving and caring for his brothers (Genesis 45), and Miriam watching over her baby brother Moses (Exodus 2:4–8).

Family relationships give insight into the relationship between God and the believers. They have a special design and importance so that they can bring honor to God.

One day, when our son Billy was eight, he decided to run away from home—"forever." He carefully packed a small suitcase with his collection of miniature animals and determinedly strode out of the house. Five minutes later he returned. "I've decided to wait until after supper." We knew the call of food would be stronger than the call of the wild! After a good meal and some laughs with us, he decided to postpone his running away indefinitely.

✗ ○ ✗

The moment had arrived; the doctor had been called. When my wife and I were making a hasty departure for the hospital, our son Tad, six, shared this parting wisdom: "Be sure and get a receipt, so if it's a girl, we can return her!"

✗ ○ ✗

Please, can I wear my pants which have the short sleeves?   JESSICA, 4

✗ ○ ✗

My sister-in-law Beth was due to give birth to her second child. As I was explaining this to my three-year-old daughter, Becky, she looked up at me with a really serious look on her face and asked, "Is Aunt Beth going to buy a girl or a boy?"

Adam, age two, didn't like orange juice because it had "things" in it, so we got a pulp-free brand; he didn't like that either because it tasted like it should have "things" in it!

X O X

I overheard this discussion between two children, a boy and a girl, in my pre-school class: The girl was quite proud as she explained that when she grew up she would have babies and be a mommy. I noticed that Tony, the little boy, looked a little downcast as he listened to her. Trying to cheer him up, I said, "Tony, when you grow up, you will be a daddy." His eyes immediately brightened as he exclaimed, "Yeah, and when I'm a daddy, then I'll drive the car!"

X O X

How come Santa has the same wrapping paper than us?   CHELSEA, 4

X O X

My four grandsons, my daughter, and I were watching a lovely French film. In it the family sat down for dinner and "la mere" placed a casserole on the table. There were "ohs" and "ahs" as the family admired the meal. My daughter sighed and said, "I wish my family reacted like that when I put dinner on the table." Four-year-old Matt patted his mom's knee and chirped, "We would, Mom, if it was peanut-butter sandwiches!"

When Katherine and Christy were about eight and six, I overheard them playing "wedding." At the point of the vows, their "minister" asked: "Do you take this woman—to take care of her when she's sick, alone, and mad?"

✗ ○ ✗

I want to be in the *Guinness Book of World Records*, Mum," Nicholas, eight, announced. "How 'bout I don't shower for a month!" SCOTLAND

✗ ○ ✗

Our neighbor's son, eleven, was departing for boarding school, tears streaming down his cheeks. His mother said, "Don't cry, David." The boy replied, "I'm not. My eyes are just juicy."

✗ ○ ✗

One summer when we were in a motel on vacation, our Mike, three, was on the bed, vigorously jumping up and down. My husband said, "Mike, you can't do that!" Not catching the message, Mike replied, "Yes, I can. Just watch" . . .and showed us again.

✗ ○ ✗

When asked what she wanted to be when she grew up, Kelly, age three, said, loud and clear, "A horse."

Ericka, five, was eating supper; she asked what she could have for dessert—ice cream, cookies, or candy. I told her, "No dessert tonight." She said, "You mean I'm eating all this stuff for nothing?"

✗ ○ ✗

Once my wife bundled up four-year-old Kimberly and sent her outside to play in the backyard. Ordinarily, we'd check to make sure the side gate was latched, but on this day we forgot to check. About a minute later, there was a knock at the back door. There stood Kimberly. "Mommy," she instructed, "you better shut the gate so I can't get out."

✗ ○ ✗

While listening to herself reciting nursery rhymes on a cassette, our three-year-old Ruthanne said, "Turn it on again. I wanna hear that kid do 'Cockle Shells'!"

✗ ○ ✗

Granddaddy," said Brooke, seven, "I have a crush on this boy at school." "Oh? So why this crush?" I asked. "Well, he's so neat—the way he looks, the way he behaves, the clothes he wears, like that." With a new week, we had a new "crush." I also asked about that: "Isn't it a little embarrassing moving from one crush to the other?" "Oh, no," Brooke answered, "I never talk to boys—just have crushes on them!"

Daddy, just this one time, won't you please *listen to me?*"   Joan, 7

✗ ○ ✗

One summer evening when Lorilynn was very small, she came in from the backyard to report that the "buzzies" were biting her. On checking, we found the area alive with mosquitoes.

✗ ○ ✗

After listening to five-year-old Christy complain several times, I sent her to her room. When I went up to talk to her on her bed, I asked if she was going to be a good little girl now. She replied, "I'm thinking. I'm just not sure about that."

✗ ○ ✗

His eldest brother got the football and ran sixty yards for a touchdown. The crowd cheered, and Torrey, four, jumped up and yelled, "That's our son!"

✗ ○ ✗

Our son Luke, four, was going downstairs with a friend who said, "We don't have stairs at our house." Luke replied, "Too bad; why doesn't your daddy buy some?"

When asked if anything ran in our family, five-year-old Alex replied, "Yes, Macky, the cat."

✗ ○ ✗

My six-year-old asked her older cousin Sarah if she had any lip gloss. Sarah said, "Yes, but you know how it is with teen sisters; you just can't never find nothing."

✗ ○ ✗

In the supermarket, Landon, three, lifted a stuffed toy out of my shopping cart. Mason, five, asked Landon for a chance to hold this toy. When his request was rejected, Mason flopped to his knees and said, "I'm gonna pray for you!" With fear in his eyes, Landon handed the toy to his brother.

✗ ○ ✗

After her little neighbor friend moved away, I asked Chelsea, four, if she was sad about this. Chelsea said, "No, I needed a vacation from her anyway."

✗ ○ ✗

Why do I like my hair so long? Well, it's like with it this way I don't have to wash behind my ears."   DENNY, 7

After an introductory discussion on the facts of life with our eight-year-old, Danielle, I said, "OK, next time we'll talk about boys." Her response, "Mommy, I'm not even eighteen yet!"

✗ ⊘ ✗

Our family had early dinner after church on Sundays, and the house was filled with extended family. After dinner my father took a nap. We all played games or read to be quiet. The bathroom was in the back of the house, and you had to pass through our parents' bedroom. One Sunday, when my eldest was four, she went to use the bathroom. As usual, Pop was sleeping in the bedroom. Soon, Pop came down laughing. She had awakened him to ask, "Pop, will it wake you if I flush the toilet?"

✗ ⊘ ✗

John and Katherine were cleaning up the family room. Christy, five, who had a stomachache, was resting in a chair. I told her brother and sister that she could help clean later, to which she responded, "Nope. I can't help. I'm going to have a stomachache all day."

✗ ⊘ ✗

Dad, we had a miracle right here in our house. When you told Lawrence to stop talking so much, he stopped!   AL, 7

Driving through a desert area of Arizona, Nina, six, needed to use a lavatory. We drove many miles before coming to a deserted roadside restaurant. I suggested Nina sneak out back. Mortified, she exclaimed, "I'm not using any fake bathroom!"

✗ ○ ✗

I asked my five-year-old granddaughter if she wanted to go to college someday. She said, "No, I want to stay home." Then I asked, "Well, what would you do after high school?" She answered, "I'd live in the basement at home. Lots of older kids do." So I said, "Well, where would you meet a husband?" Jenny said, "At home." "Well, where will you and your husband live after you get married?" Jenny said, "Right here at home."

✗ ○ ✗

When his mother spanked him, five-year-old Tory said, "That didn't hurt." His mother replied, "I can spank harder." Tory quickly responded, "No, that first one will make me behave."

✗ ○ ✗

Our five-year-old granddaughter was looking at pictures of my daughter's three dogs. She said, "They're my dog cousins."

Our nephew Peter, six, was trying, in vain, to teach his elderly aunt to play chess. Finally, exasperated, he said, "Neemee, someone else'll have to show you, 'cause I just can't get through to you!"

✗ ○ ✗

Our grandson David, four, was born with a digestive problem that called for some special attention around the house. One day, his five-year-old sister said, "I don't care if you love David more than me; he's so tiny."

✗ ○ ✗

Shhhh. Mommy, when you come in this room, whisper with your feet. My dolls are sleeping.   BONNIE, 4 (CHINA)

✗ ○ ✗

My teen brother and his friends smoke cigarettes in their tree hut out back. I told my mother, who said she'd tell my father. Well *I'm* gonna tell God, even if He already knows. He's so busy; I'm gonna remind Him.

DONNA, 10

✗ ○ ✗

At bedtime, I told our little Luke that he had a good heart. "Where is it?" he asked. "Maybe in my pajamas?"

When I was a pilot, I gave my kids and grandkids rides in my plane. Once Caleb, age six, said he remembered when he rode in my plane. I reminded him that the only ride he made with me was when he was still in his mama's tummy. He replied, "I know that, but I still remember. Don't you remember when you turned and the wing went down on one side? Well, that's when I slid down and bumped my head on one of Mama's ribs. Boy! That really hurt, too."

XOX

When my boys were very little, Donny came in to report Bobby, three, was ill. "Mommy, Mommy, Bobby just spilled his appetite!"

XOX

Toddler Niki had heard the expression, "If you can't run with the older dogs, stay on the porch." During a roughhouse session on the bed with Dad and Mom, Niki's older sister felt she was getting too much roughing and complained. Whereupon, Niki indignantly said to Nina, "If you can't play with the big dogs. . .uh, then go play with the little dogs."

XOX

Julie, three, had been naughty. As her dad scolded her, he asked her, "Julie, tell me, why did you do that?" Her response: "Because I'm just a naughty kid."

When her little brother was born, our three-year-old granddaughter, Karlita, spent the night with us. "Where did the baby come from?" she asked. "From God," I replied. "Yes," she said, "but how did He get to the hospital?" I said, "Honey, when you get a little older, you'll understand." Karlita leaned over close to me and said, "Grandma, if you talk a little louder, I can understand you right now."

✗ ○ ✗

Exasperated by a never-ceasing barrage of questions from Ken, seven, my husband said, "I just don't know the answer to that one, Son." The youngster responded, "Well, that sounds like a good excuse!"

✗ ○ ✗

I told young Justus to go upstairs and get dressed. After a bit, I went upstairs and there he was, still in his underpants. I said, "Why aren't you dressed?" He said, "I am dressed." I said, "Dressing means more than just underpants. You need clothes—pants and shirt." Justus: "I am dressed. My clothes, Mom, are just invisible."

✗ ○ ✗

Christopher, five, just couldn't wait to be six. Why? "Because then I'll be bigger and can reach way up to the cookie jar!"

Once I chose a family gathering to show off my new, slim waistline. When I stood up and took in a deep breath, my trousers fell down to my ankles. When we next visited the family, our five-year-old granddaughter, Karen, said "My Sunday school teacher was surprised when I told him you took off your pants at dinner."

$$\times \, o \, \times$$

My first night home after YWCA camp, I told my mom that the worst dinner they had there was pork, applesauce, and Jell-O for dessert. That night Mom's "welcome home" dinner was pork, applesauce, and Jell-O!

SARA, 10

$$\times \, o \, \times$$

One day we were with my nephews, Keith and Chad. We were driving back to Nana and Paw Paw's house following lunch at the boys' favorite place, McDonalds. We asked the boys what they wanted to be when they grew up. Without hesitation, Chad, three, piped up, "I want to be a McDonalds' cooker!"

$$\times \, o \, \times$$

When the proud parents told their twin girls that another child was expected, they said, "Oh, we can't; there are only four places for toothbrushes."

Jimmy's parents decided it was time to advise little Jimmy that a new baby would arrive by Christmas. Not knowing exactly how to break the news, they decided to take the indirect approach. They asked, "Jim, if you had a choice, which would you rather have, a baby sister or a baby brother?" Little Jimmy replied, "I'd rather have a baby pony."

xox

While sitting on her dad's lap reading, Rachel, four, asked to see Daddy's chest. She lifted up his shirt, then lifted up her blouse. After a comparison, she stated, "I don't have grass on my chest!"

xox

Six-year-old Len wiped away his tears after a spanking, regained his composure, and said, "OK, now that we have that taken care of, are we goin' to the circus Saturday, or not?"

xox

Because he had disobeyed, our five-year-old son was crying softly. A few minutes later he said, "Why was I crying? I don't know. Maybe I'll figure that out tomorrow."

I asked four-year-old Beth why she was being so crabby. She replied, "I'm just tired of being four years old!"

XOX

Yesterday, Beth woke up at 5:00 A.M. I urged her to go back to sleep, but she said, "I can't. I got a life to live!"

XOX

In an upbeat mood about his sister, Ethan, four, said, "I like her so much that when we both grow up, we will marry together."

XOX

Feeling just a bit exasperated with my daughter Audrey, six, I said, "Will you please be quiet!" Without pause, she said, "I can't. I'm still talking."

XOX

One day, I asked our daughter if she'd help me do some chores around the house, because I couldn't get it all done before dinner. Her reply: "Mom, you seem to be doing OK without me."

When I saw my four-year-old, David, wandering around with a very soiled toothbrush, I asked, "What have you been doing with that toothbrush—cleaning the bathroom floor?" "Yes," he replied.

✗ ○ ✗

Our four-year-old was playing a computer game. When he lost, his sister, twelve, pretended to cry. Our son's response: "Melanie, please don't cry. You make me nervous, and besides, it's only a game."

✗ ○ ✗

When I told Amanda, five, that she was going to have a baby sister or brother in the summer, she said, "Oh, good; right now let's go tell Mommy!"

✗ ○ ✗

Sporting his very first two-piece dress suit, our grandson said to his sister, "Now that I've got this preacher suit, Tracie, I suppose I can't lie to you anymore."

✗ ○ ✗

At the beach, our eldest granddaughter said, "Oh, look! A jellyfish!" Then her little sister DeAndre, three, leaned down, studied the water, and searched for a peanut-butter fish!

During my pregnancy, Julie, age four, had many questions: "Did God put the baby in your stomach? Does God know if the baby has hair? Is it a boy or a girl?" I tried to answer all these questions. Finally I said, "Yes, dear, God knows all of these things." Then she asked, "Well, if He knows all about the baby, please pull up your shirt and let me see the window God looks through."

TWISTED WORDS

Our dog, named Nicodemus, was forever licking three-year-old Kati's face. So when someone asked the dog's name, she appropriately replied, "Lickademus."

Our young grandson Andy said, "Let's sing that Christmas song: '. . . and heaven and nature seen.' "

Ryan, five, said, "Daddy, sing that duck-tail song." Perplexed, I said, "What song?" He sang, "Duck-tail halls with boughs of holly."

"I assure you,
anyone who doesn't have
their kind of faith
will never get into
the Kingdom of God."
Then he took the children
into his arms and placed his hands
on their heads and blessed them.

MARK 10:15–16

3

God

X O X

Don't worry, Grandma, up here on this Ferris wheel
we're much closer to God!

DANIEL, 5

Children form special relationships with those who love and value them. They know to whom they can turn for help. Sometimes their mothers or fathers even come without being called. The same is true with their relationship with God. When they learn about God and His love for them at an early age, a strong attachment to their heavenly Father begins to grow.

To children, God is not merely a spirit who is invisible or mysterious. To them, He is a friend, a helper, a protector, a partner in their daily activities. They know God is a part of whatever is going on. They trust their parents, so they know God can be trusted, too.

Since children view the world through the lenses of their own experiences, their explanations of God and His character are in their own terms. Their insights, as demonstrated in this chapter, are sweet, humorous, and thought-provoking. Children, with their trusting natures, can be powerful examples of what it means to incorporate God into our daily activities and enjoy fellowship with Him.

At age six, Lorilynn made a Christmas list for Santa: a black sweater, a box of candy, a box of modeling clay, barrettes, hair bands, ribbons, and so on. Ribbons were then thoughtfully crossed off with this note beside it: "Oops, God already gave them to me."

✗ ○ ✗

On a starry night, our five-year-old son, Simon, looked at the sky and said, "Look how nice the wallpaper is God's got in His house."

✗ ○ ✗

Jonathan, four, reported in Sunday school class the teacher said Jesus healed blind Bartimaeus. Later she said that *God* healed Bartimaeus. Jonathan immediately said, "I thought you said Jesus healed Bartimaeus." The teacher replied, "But Jesus is God." After class, when the other kids were deciding what crayon to draw with, Jonathan, concerned with other things, asked the teacher, "How could God be His own Son?"

✗ ○ ✗

In 1956, soon after the sinking of the passenger ship SS *Andrea Doria*, we were en route to the Holy Land on the SS *Constitution*. Our son, David, five, commented, "I don't care if this boat sinks. I'm just glad God's let me live this long!"

Our daughter Nora, six, called into the bathroom, "What are you doing in there?" "I just took a nice, clean shower," I answered. Her comment: "Good. God always wants us to be nice and clean."

✗ ○ ✗

Our seven-year-old son had finished listening to a sermon about giving account of ourselves on the Day of Judgment. After we came home from church, he was busy memorizing his multiplication. He looked up and said, "When the Lord asks me what three times nine is, I want to be able to give Him the right answer."

✗ ○ ✗

That kid, Leroy, who sits next to me in history class, is such a dork," said our third-grader, Vince. "But our Sunday school teacher says God loves everybody. Even dorks?"

✗ ○ ✗

We have three kids under nine. So when our mealtime discussions gravitate toward God, we never quite know where they'll end up. Last night, David, seven, was saying God doesn't make adults. "He specializes in babies, and the reason He makes just little boys and girls is because He doesn't have to really take care of them, you see. He lets the mommies and daddies do that."

Some years ago, our young nephew was enrolled in a vacation Bible school at a local church. As he returned home each day, his mother would ask him what had gone on that particular day. One day, the entire group had been taken to the church sanctuary, where the minister took them on a tour and talked to the kids about the worship services and ministries of the church. That afternoon, when asked the usual question by his mother, he said, "Oh, today we went to visit God's house. God wasn't there, but we did talk with His manager."

✗ ⭕ ✗

There was a low bank of fog on the day we took the trip around New York City's harbor. As the enshrouded Statue of Liberty came into view, our grandson Mike, four, was in awe and said, "Look, look there, it's God!"

✗ ⭕ ✗

According to our grandson Josh, seven, God's last name is "Forbid."

FRANCE

✗ ⭕ ✗

Our young grandson gave this "sermon" at youth church: "When my sister's being a pain in the neck, lots of times I ask God to make her behave. And sometimes He does. Cool."

Gail, three, was shopping with her mother. While they were waiting in line at the checkout counter, a lady walked up to Gail and asked, "Where did you get those big brown eyes?" Looking as though she couldn't understand why anyone would ask such a question, Gail said, "Of course, from God!"

X O X

Do you think God likes my new "Jesus Loves You" bracelet?   LINDA, 6

X O X

Looking at the sky at dusk, I said to Tom (seven): "God paints such a beautiful sunset." Tom said, "And He does it all with His left hand, because Jesus is sitting on His right hand."

X O X

When my brother passed away suddenly last month, our five-year-old daughter, in a pensive mood, asked, "Dad, Uncle Harry was such a nice guy. Why did God let him die?"

X O X

For no apparent reason, six-year-old Annie said, "OK, so God made kids, but I think His best invention is my Game Boy."

One morning in children's church, after records were recorded, the director was preparing to take the children into adult church. As she was lining up the children to march into the church, she noticed my little nephew was crying. She asked him why he was crying—what was wrong. Through his tears, he informed her that he could not go into church because he had given all his money in the offering in children's church. When she explained that all the money was put together and was used for God's work and in telling others about Jesus, he immediately dried his tears, and, with a big smile, marched into church.

✗ ○ ✗

If God had a refrigerator, He'd have my picture on the door.   ALLAN, 7

✗ ○ ✗

God, if You look real carefully at me over at Sandy's birthday party on Saturday, You'll see my new sneakers.   SONYA, 5

✗ ○ ✗

Brent, fifteen, had some money from his paper route, and I took him to buy a couple of shirts. We happened on a good sale, and he was able to buy several nice shirts. As we drove home, Brent said, "Yahweh always blesses me so much."

I hear God loves everyone, but the thing is—He's never met my sister.

ARNOLD, 8

✗ O ✗

Ethan, four, interrupted his play frequently one night to run to Mom and Dad and Grandpa and Grandma to plant a kiss on one of us (whoever he could reach) and exclaim, "I love you!" Grandma and Grandpa asked, "You are so full of 'mush' and love tonight. Where did you get this wonderful gift?" Ethan paused in thought for a moment, then said "God gave it to me!" Then he jumped off my lap and ran off to play.

✗ O ✗

Hey, I know lightning is God's flashlight. . .but thunder? Well, I guess that's His voice!

ERIC, 8

✗ O ✗

Describing something really tall, Chris, age six, said, "It's all the way up to God's feet!"

✗ O ✗

I got an "Answer Man" toy machine from a fast-food place. I asked the machine, "How did they make God?" The answer: "Don't know. Try again."

JOSH, 8

God must get awful tired on Sunday mornings trying to get everybody up, dressed, and to church on time.   RONNIE, 6

✗ O ✗

Aunt Sherrill asked Stacey, three, "Who made the sky, the flowers, grass, and clouds?" Stacey answered, "God did." And when asked, "And who made you?" Stacey said, "I don't know." So Aunt Sherrill said, "God did." Stacey replied, "Oh, wasn't that nice of Him!"

✗ O ✗

My eight-year-old granddaughter, Jenna, was being taken care of by a twelve-year-old baby-sitter. Both these girls are from divorced families. Cece, the sitter, asked Jenna: "How many dads do you have?" Jenna responded, "Two." Cece replied, "So who is your second dad?" "My father in Kentucky," (her biological father) said Jenna. "Then who is your first dad?" asked Cece. "God," was my granddaughter's wise reply.

✗ O ✗

In 1993, the city of Bettendorf, Iowa, was flooded. My great granddaughter Heather, age five, was worried. So I told her God would never destroy the world again with a flood. Then she asked, "Not even in Bettendorf?"

On a picnic day, it looked like rain in the morning, but cleared up by afternoon. Three-year-old Kate said, "When God got up this morning and looked at His list, He saw 'picnic,' so He stopped the rain and made the sky blue." IRELAND

✗ o ✗

My son Ryan, ten, and his dad were having a conversation about how God plays an active role in our lives, and how things that happen to us are under God's control. After thinking a moment, Ryan answered, "We are like action figures for God!"

✗ o ✗

While riding the Ferris wheel at a school-sponsored event, five-year-old Daniel and I were at the top when the wheel stopped turning. I confided that I had forgotten how it felt on a Ferris wheel and that my favorite ride was the merry-go-round. Daniel saw my fear and said, "Don't worry, Grandma, up here we're much closer to God."

✗ o ✗

While driving in the Smoky Mountains, we ran into a rain shower. Brett, five, said seriously, "Isn't God good? He sent the rain just to wash our windshield!"

Brittany, four, was in a Christian day care center. Before the children went downstairs to the sanctuary to practice their Christmas program, the director said that they needed to be on their best behavior when they went to God's house. While downstairs, the director saw Brittany looking around. Asked what she was looking for, Brittany said, "God. I was hoping that He'd be home today!"

XOX

When my two grandsons were three and four years old, I kept them for six weeks while their mom recuperated from surgery. The older one's fifth birthday came during that time. His mother called to make sure he had a special day, because she said this was really important to him. I made the day very special and, of course, ended it with cake and ice cream. The boys were so hyped up that I didn't know whether I would ever get them calm enough to go to sleep. As I was trying to get them settled in bed, a real bad electrical storm blew in. Damon jumped up and pulled the curtain back and said, "Look, Grandma, even God is wishing me happy birthday." Then he rolled over on his tummy and went to sleep!

Hey, God is the "Great Maker." He, by Himself, made the earth, the sea, the trees—all that stuff; the fish, the birds, the animals—big and small; and He made the people—everywhere. He loves us all. Especially kids. And that's why I love Him!

TOMMY, 8 (CANADA)

TWISTED WORDS

Amy, two, has a distinctly phonetic vocabulary:
perfume is "perfoon";
tulips are "lipsticks";
a Kleenex is a "blownex";
and oatmeal? Of course, that's "oakmilk cereal"!

Know what a myth is?
A kind of girl moth.
DENISE, 5

Our middle daughter calls a hippopotamus a "hoppingbottom."

Children are a gift from the LORD;
they are a reward from him.

PSALM 127:3

A wise child brings joy to a father;
a foolish child brings grief to a mother.

PROVERBS 10:1

4

Parents

X O X

*They're like countless yards of fabric woven together,
making a pattern of love and kindness.*

CAROLINE, 9

Children look past the faults or shortcomings of their mothers or fathers and esteem their parents as the most wonderful persons in the world. They strive to imitate their actions, and talk and act like they do. Who hasn't seen a little girl struggling to walk in her mother's high heels? Or a boy riding on his tricycle pretending to be Daddy driving the car? By watching their parents, children are learning about life and what is important to them. Parents have a God-given opportunity to mold and train their children at this young age and to instill in them godly principles. After all, the Bible instructs parents to "train a child in the way he should go, and when he is old he will not turn from it" (Proverbs 22:6 NIV).

I was visiting my daughter-in-law a few days ago, and she was telling me that she was talking about birth order with her four-year-old daughter, Jacqueline. Jacqueline looked up at her mother and said, "Daddy was your first baby born, wasn't he, Mommy?"

✗ O ✗

Yves, seven, sent this letter to his parents from camp. "Dear Mom and Dad: Please don't worry about me, because I'm not worried about you. I want to thank you so much for the package you didn't send me yet."

SWITZERLAND

✗ O ✗

Six-year-old Simon said, "Dad is the only one with good ideas on what to do on Sunday afternoons, but he always thinks of them on Mondays!"

✗ O ✗

We had just moved into a new house, and four-year-old Todd was frightened in his new bedroom. One night he crawled into bed with us, crying, "There's a gorilla in my room." We assured him there was no gorilla, but that we would watch for the gorilla just in case, and he was to go back to sleep. Within a few seconds, both of us dropped off to sleep, only to be awakened by his fearful scream: "You're not watching!"

While on a walk, our nine-year-old, Bill, asked, "How far is a country mile?" Before I had a chance to answer, his younger brother said, "It's sort of like our dad's minute!"

One evening as I was putting my daughter to bed, she wanted to know how Daddy and Mommy met and got married. After hearing our courtship/wedding story and thinking it over, she looked up at me and said, "I'm never getting married, even if you drive me there."

When Jeremy was three, he was fascinated with his mother's nursing of Baby Devon. Jeremy asked his brother if he could feed Devon. Scott replied, "Silly; I don't have the right plumbing."

Young David accompanied his parents to the adoption agency for the arrival of his new baby sister. He sat quietly in the reception area looking at another couple with their new baby. When the social worker asked how he liked his new sister, he said, "Fine, but why didn't you give us one with some hair like the one out in the other room?"

Jodi was enjoying her new tricycle when her big brother, Rick, asked if he could ride it. She said, "No." So Rick told her, "I don't love you anymore." Jodi replied, "Maybe not, but Mommy do."

X O X

At the first clap of thunder, six-year-old Brian climbed trembling into bed with his mom. After a short period of comforting and reassurance, Mom suggested that it was time for Brian to return to his own bed in order to make room for Daddy. "Is Daddy afraid, too? The big sissy!"

X O X

My mom does everything at our house. She gives the dog a bath—us, too. She drives me to the dentist; she cooks dinner in the microwave; she makes us kids be good. And Dad? Well, he carries in the groceries.   PEGGY, 4

X O X

In an effort to keep Braeden, two, in bed at night, his parents gave him a choice of keeping one toy or one book with him. So this night, after hearing Mommy's "makeup" stories, she asked, "Braeden, which do you want to keep in bed with you tonight—a book or a toy?" Thinking a moment, he responded, "I want Mommy."

When Christina was only three years old, I sent her into the bedroom to awaken her father from a nap. When she didn't return, I went and found her trying to lift her father's eyelid. Seeing me, she quickly explained, "I was just looking to see if he's really in there."

X O X

Pascal, eight, said, "Mom, if you and Dad were not born, I would be an orphan." FRANCE

X O X

On our tenth wedding anniversary card, our first-grader wrote: "I can't belev you bin marred so long. Anyhow, I love you!"

X O X

Commenting on the pastor's reference to our fiftieth wedding anniversary, our little niece asked, "What's all that 'holy monotony' stuff he was talking about?"

X O X

Out of the blue, our daughter Melissa, three, said, "When I grow up, I'm going to be a mommy, carry a purse, and wonder where to go."

My mom was telling me about getting born. Whew! Tough. I wish I'd grown out of the ground like a carrot. That's what Henry next door did.

JASON, 5

✗ ⊘ ✗

Rushing home from the maternity ward, my husband was welcomed at the door by our four-year-old daughter. Bursting with pride and joy, he exclaimed, "Guess what? Mommy just had a baby; now you have a baby brother!" The new big sister replied, "Oh, dear, I was hoping it would be a baby kitty."

✗ ⊘ ✗

My husband was joking about the frequency of my hair permanents at the beauty parlor when our ten-year-old daughter chimed in, "Mom, you get so many perms, Dad's starting to call them 'temporaries!'" ENGLAND

✗ ⊘ ✗

One day, I lost my temper with our four-year-old twins because of their unwillingness to help when I asked them to do small jobs. I sat them down for a talk and reasoned, "If you wanted me to help you with something like buttoning your pants or fixing something, and I said 'no,' wouldn't you feel kind of angry with me?" David quickly said, "Yes, but I would forgive you!"

Looking to the future, Stavros, age eight, said, "Even after I get married, I'm going to live with Mommy and Daddy." Her sister asked, "Well, what if your husband says you have to move away with him?" Stavros answered, "Easy. I'll just kick him out!"

✗ ○ ✗

I heard our daughter Judy and her friend talking while playing dolls. "I'll just bet you've got to mind your dad; he's the boss in your house. Right?" her friend said. "Well, yes, unless my mama's around," Judy answered.

✗ ○ ✗

We'd just brought our new baby home from the hospital. A day or two later, I stepped outside for some fresh air, leaving the baby inside with her daddy and sister Kate. Moments later, Kate opened the front door and with a firm voice called out, "Your baby is crying in my house!"

✗ ○ ✗

Anticipating a weeklong, beachside family reunion, our grown daughter was stressed about getting trim and thin to look good in a bathing suit. Our grandson Justin crawled onto her lap, put his arms around her, and said, "Oh, no, Mom, we like you blubbery just the way you are!"

I was explaining to Kyle, six, that I was going to Washington, D.C. on a special business trip where I would meet the president of the United States. He excitedly exclaimed, "Wow, you're going to meet George Washington!"

✗ ⦿ ✗

While driving in Los Angeles, I told my husband, "Watch out. That light's about to turn red." From the backseat, our five-year-old daughter, Carol, said, "Oh, he doesn't pay any attention to those."

✗ ⦿ ✗

Grumbling about her chores, Nina, six, said, "Mom, you're treating me like Cinderella."

✗ ⦿ ✗

My patience waning, I said to our son Alstair, "Now, don't you argue with me!" To which he retorted, "OK, Mother, then don't you argue with me!"

✗ ⦿ ✗

On a bus into town one day, my four-year-old asked me in a loud, clear voice, "Mom, why don't you want any more of us kids?"

I'm just a little child, but my mother watches over me. She's so loving and caring. But I know how she feels when I get mad at her. But that's all right because she's my mother, and I love her and I know that she loves me.

BREANNA, 10

✗ ⭕ ✗

Ryan, two, was terribly upset one evening when being left with his grand-mother. She finally put him in his crib, where he sobbed and sobbed, "I want my mama. I want my dada. I so mad!"

✗ ⭕ ✗

I preached at the morning church service and was scheduled again for the evening program. I was looking forward to a restful Sunday afternoon, but this was interrupted abruptly by the arrival of our two young grandchildren and three-year-old Nancy from next door. In a flash, my time of relaxation ended with the cry, "Grandpa, let's wrestle!" Before long, I was pinned to the carpet. Later, I collapsed on the couch to rest with little Nancy. "I'd have fun," she told me, "if you'd be my daddy." Later, I learned this love-starved little girl didn't have a daddy.

✗ ⭕ ✗

They're like countless yards of fabric woven together, making a pattern of love and kindness.

CAROLINE, 9

Then Jesus prayed this prayer:
"O Father, Lord of heaven and earth,
thank you for hiding the truth
from those who think
themselves so wise and clever,
and for revealing it to the childlike."

MATTHEW 11:25

5

Jesus

X O X

I believe in Jesus,
because He's nice and He put me here.

Bart, 5

Children identify with Jesus in a special way because He experienced the same things they do. Jesus was born as a baby, just as they were. Jesus was a little child and grew up in a home with His parents, just as they do. We celebrate His birthday every year, just as they have a birthday. The Savior of the world understands just what it is like to be a child!

As they grow older, children learn of the sacrifice Jesus made when He gave His life on the cross, and their love for Him grows. Here is a friend who gave up all He had for their sake.

In this world, children are often overlooked. Adults rush around taking care of their busy schedules and don't take time to listen to kids or just "hang out" with them. But Jesus said clearly that children are important to Him. He always has time for them.

Jesus is God's Son, you know. And lots of times on the little stuff usually I pray like this: "Jesus, please help me behave better in my social studies class, even if Mrs. Simpson doesn't like me." Jesus helped me with that one, and He didn't even have to check it out with His Father.

WESLEY, 6 (SOUTH AFRICA)

✗ O ✗

My daughter Kelly, five, and I were visiting our friend Charlotte who gave Kelly a tour of the five large rooms of her apartment. Kelly said, "This is so big! Who lives here with you, Aunt Charlotte?" "I live here alone," Charlotte replied. Kelly thought for a moment and then said, "Oh, but you're not really alone 'cause you have Jesus!"

✗ O ✗

Our twelve-year-old daughter was lamenting the fact that she seems to spend all of her allowance: "Spend, spend, I never save." Overhearing this, her younger brother commented, "Jesus saves; why can't you?"

✗ O ✗

I told my daughter Cheri to stop digging around in the 'fridge and close its door. She responded, "I think Jesus told me to keep digging around in there and get some cherries."

This guy in my homeroom at school has got it all wrong. He thinks he's cool, 'cause he's got a new ten-speed bike and is going to baseball camp. But he says he's an atheist, doesn't even believe in Jesus. And that's not cool.

JERRY, 9

✗ O ✗

Immediately after six-year-old Brent was saved, he started telling his friends about Jesus. One day Brent's mom took him to get a haircut. Into the barber shop walked a tough-looking guy with long, dirty hair and a tattoo. Brent whispered to his mom, "Did you know I tell all my friends about Jesus?" She replied, "Yes." Brent continued, "Then don't you think you should talk to that man about Jesus?"

✗ O ✗

Our Katherine, age five, went with us to see a musical of the Christmas story. She was so enraptured with the actors that played Mary and Joseph that when the baby Jesus was born in the manger, she wanted to know what they named Him!

✗ O ✗

Let's go to the beach, Dad. I want to take walking lessons so I can walk on the water like Jesus.

BEN, 4

Jesus hears everything, my mom says—everything. I guess He must have some way of shutting off the junk on TV, the radio, and stuff so He can hear me and my brother's prayers.   KEVIN, 5

✗ O ✗

Every time I get in trouble at home, I get sent to my room. Then my mom forgives me. But more important, so does Jesus!   HENRY, 6

✗ O ✗

It was a spectacular event—our town's Fourth of July celebration with multi-colored fireworks rocketing across the sky. In total awe, our seven-year-old granddaughter, Brooke, exclaimed, "Oh, I do hope Jesus is enjoying this!"

✗ O ✗

My daughter was about three when I was telling her about Adam and Eve being very naughty and eating the apple God told them not to eat. "Oh," said little Nancy, "don't worry, Mommy, I wouldn't eat anything Jesus didn't cook."

✗ O ✗

The Bible says Jesus is amazing. He loves every boy and girl who loves Him—even my sister, who's always driving me nuts.   ROB, 6

When I asked my five-year-old, Rick, why he was talking to himself, he answered, "I'm not talking to me. I'm talking to Jesus; telling Him what I want to hear."

✗ O ✗

Sometimes, if I'm sad when I pray, on my cheek comes a little tear. I always feel better then, 'cause that tear makes me feel Jesus is near.

HEIDI, 9 (GERMANY)

✗ O ✗

Does Jesus still do miracles? You bet He does. Like my sister Evie (who always bugs me) didn't want to leave me alone. But last week He sent her to Girl Scout camp.

THOMAS, 7

✗ O ✗

I believe in Jesus, because He's nice and He put me here. Also, anytime He wants He can take me to heaven; but not yet, I hope.

BART, 5 (WALES)

✗ O ✗

Mom, the thing is if you and Dad ever get me a brother, let's name him Jesus, 'cause then we know he'll always be a good kid.

BETSY, 5

So, coming home from Macy's Thanksgiving Day Parade with my dad, sitting near us on the subway was this very old man. He looked sad, so I was praying Jesus would make him feel better. Well, he picked up a newspaper off the floor, started reading it, and all of a sudden he smiled. Well, you know I think Jesus put a cheerful, funny something in that paper. Amen!

VANESSA, 10

✗ O ✗

Four kindergarten children were seated around a table working on an art project. The teacher overheard one of them say, "I know the devil is red and lives down there" (pointing to the floor). Then Megan spoke up, "My mother says Jesus lives up here—in my heart."

✗ O ✗

When our daughter Jenny was four, she loved to have her bath at night. We would chatter about many things, but always about how much Jesus loved her. One evening, Jenny announced that she would like to invite Jesus to come into her heart. I was thrilled, but said, "Are you sure, Jenny?" She answered, "Yes, I really am!" So I took her little hand and got ready to pray with her. Suddenly, Jenny sat straight up on the tub and said: "Wait! Wait! Wait! Wait!" Startled, I responded: "What's the matter, Jenny? Don't you want to invite Jesus into your heart?" Jenny replied: "Yes, but I'm afraid to ask Him into my heart cuz He might get stuck in my throat!"

I think Jesus did lots of miracles on babies and children like my little sister, because it's easier to make miracles in them than in big kids like me.

GRETCHEN, 8

✗ O ✗

At a family celebration of my eightieth birthday, our five-year-old grand-daughter, Kim, announced, "Good news: Grandma'll get to see Jesus before the rest of us guys."

✗ O ✗

We asked our son Adam, two, what was the meaning of Christmas. Holding three fingers, he said, "It's Jesus' birthday, and this year He's going to be three!"

✗ O ✗

When we asked Justus, six, if he'd say grace at dinner, he said, "Sure, no problem. Dear God, thank You for giving us the baby Jesus, so He could die for us, and we could always have love in our hearts."

✗ O ✗

For our very young granddaughter, desserts are the best part of every meal. "Do you think Jesus will have desserts in heaven?" she once asked.

Our sons, aged three and five, were taking a bath together. "I'm walking on water, just like Jesus," said the younger one. The older brother: "You are walking in water, not on water. Now, sit down!"

✗ O ✗

This guy at school was saying, "Know what you're born for? To die—just born to die." I said, "OK, but if you meet Jesus along the way, you'll live forever in heaven."   KAREN, 9

✗ O ✗

Our grandchildren were having great fun playing with plastic glow-in-the-dark bugs we'd given them. Christopher, five, said, "Grandma, this is like Jesus; if we stay close to Him, we will glow in the dark! Right?"

✗ O ✗

During a children's service, our pastor asked what's brown, furry, and jumps from tree to tree? A little boy answered, "Normally, I would say a squirrel, but since you asked the question, I guess it must be Jesus."   NORWAY

"Dad," said our daughter Susan, nine, "can you just imagine the many ways Jesus can call His disciples today? By phone, by fax, by E-mail, by cell phone, or even by an overnight letter delivered by UPS!"

TWISTED WORDS

Grandson Cody used to call
his canker sores his "cranky sores."

Four-year-old David told me
the moral of the story was,
"Two heads are bigger than one."

Our four-year-old, Caitlin, said,
"Santa Claus is coming tonight,
and he's bringing all the presidents."

"There's a young boy here
with five barley loaves and two fish.
But what good is that
with this huge crowd?"

JOHN 6:9

6

Outreach

X O X

*Kids in missions,
the church, and Sunday school*

Webster's Dictionary defines "outreach" as "to go beyond." And that's exactly what this chapter's all about: how kids observe this going beyond through their personal experience, their "walk" in the world of mission, the church, and the Sunday school.

I've been a missionary kid for my whole life. I could write many pages about what kids think (or, at least, what I think!) about missions. While there's no set formula for predicting how a child will cope with being a missionary's kid, you can know all of us in the field are committed to sharing the great story of God and His Word worldwide. Adapting to new cultures is sometimes not easy, but we have a ministry to carry out.

Children are an important part of every church. Besides providing welcome comic relief, children are the future of the church. They are the future pastors, missionaries, deacons, elders, Sunday school teachers. While today they are young and immature, in just a few short years they will have to take their places of authority and responsibility in the church. Therefore, their participation in the activities of the church is valuable, not just because we can be amused by their antics, but because their antics are a part of growing into mature human beings, ready to live for Christ.

Jesus didn't say, "Let the little children come to me" because He needed a laugh. He said this because He cared about children—their minds, thoughts, questions. He didn't dismiss them because they were young; rather, He welcomed them, blessed them. He felt kids mattered. Finally, He recognized that people of all ages have a child's mind when compared with God, and that a child has the benefit of innocence and sees things through eyes untainted by a lifetime of sin.

Jesus' parents once found Him in the Temple listening to the teachers. Young Jesus asked, "Why were you searching for me? Didn't you know I had to be in my Father's house?" (Luke 2:41–50 NIV). This is one of history's earliest instances of a little boy speaking about a place of worship. In the pages to follow are the voices of today's children speaking to today's adults.

JUSTIN B. HOPKINS, *Dakar Academy, in Dakar, Senegal; son of Brad and Betsy Hopkins, missionaries with Wycliffe Bible Translators*

Explaining why she didn't think her new Sunday school class was going to go very well, Stephanie, age nine, said, "Too many wild crows in one nest."

✗ ○ ✗

Missionaries should go to the North Pole, because Santa Claus doesn't know about Jesus.   KATE, 4

✗ ○ ✗

When we returned to our seats after being served communion at the altar, our two-year-old daughter said, "I want some crackers, too!"

✗ ○ ✗

Our church's Celebration Bell Ringers performed at two Christmas services, at the second of which my young niece said, "Oh, great! The ringers are re-belling!"

✗ ○ ✗

Julie, four, was asking where our real home is. I told her we have two homes, one in America, and one in Taiwan. She quickly added, "And one in heaven!"   TAIWAN

On arriving in Japan, we first stayed at our mission headquarters in Tokyo. During our first bus ride, our four-year-old daughter, Pam, whispered, "Look, Daddy, all the people have black hair and brown eyes." JAPAN

✗ ○ ✗

You should always go to Sunday school, even if you'd have more fun at the beach. Hey, the beach is better in the afternoon and, besides, it might be cloudy all day. ART, 7

✗ ○ ✗

For some reason, at age three, Jonathan was afraid when flying in an airplane. After his baby sister, Sarah, was born in Ferkessedougou, Ivory Coast, the family was flying back to the Operation Mobilization missionary ship on which they were serving. After they took off, Jonathan told his daddy he was afraid. "Why are you afraid?" asked his dad. "Because I might fall out, and Ferkessedougou is very hard!" WEST AFRICA

✗ ○ ✗

During our missionary career, we had often lived in one or two rooms in group housing, so when we moved into a five-room apartment on furlough, our four-year-old said, "Who else is going to live here?"

In Sunday school, a week after we arrived in the States on missionary furlough, our four-year-old, Kenneth, was asked to write his name, his address, and his father's job on the blackboard. So he wrote, "Ken. Africa. A cop." The teacher said, "Your dad's a cop?" "No, he's really a missionary, but I can't spell that."

✗ ○ ✗

One of our Sunday school teachers asked her little children as they were on the way to a special church service, "Why is it necessary to be quiet in church?" One little girl replied, "Because people are sleeping."

✗ ○ ✗

We live in Iowa, but when we were talking about our church's new building program, our son Tom, seven, said, "To get more people to come, let's just build it in the middle of Disneyland."

✗ ○ ✗

Now, here's the thing: I have this friend next door. Her name's Kim. She told me she doesn't believe in God. Once I took her to Sunday school. Now, she goes with me every Sunday, and now she says she loves Jesus. My mother says maybe someday I can be a missionary. I'd like that.   MARCIA, 8

A group of kids were comparing notes about school. One said, "I'm starting first grade." Another, "My mom homeschools me, and I'm in third." Not to be left out, Ben, four, added, "I'm in Sunday school!"

XOX

Our daughter Sara, five, once said to her maiden great-aunt, "I know lots of guys would like to be your husbands, but, Auntie, they just don't know where you go to church."

XOX

Victoria, two, was standing on the bench at church. During the preaching she started singing "Jesus Loves Me." She was dipping her shoulders one at a time, bending her knees, and singing at the top of her voice, much to the embarrassment of her mother but the delight of the assembly!

XOX

When my granddaughter Anna was two years old, her dad conducted a baptism one Sunday morning. Someone asked, "Anna, what happened at church today?" She replied, "Nothin', just my daddy preached in the water and washed a lady's hair."

After her first day in Sunday school, our little Lynn, four, said, "The girls are nice to the boys, and the boys are mean to the girls, and that's sure the way it is."

✗ ∂ ✗

Arriving on furlough in mid-school year, Paul began his second semester of third grade. His teacher asked, "What does your daddy do?" Paul answered, "My daddy doesn't do anything. He's a missionary."

✗ ∂ ✗

One of the charter members from my home church was preparing her "kiddies" for their annual step-up into the next grade when one kindergartner asked, "When is our teacher, Miss Dottie, going to graduate?"

✗ ∂ ✗

You know you're a missionary kid if you flew before you could walk; you see pictures of friends in the *National Geographic;* you dream of a green Christmas; you learn to pack your clothes, fast; you find out a furlough is no vacation; your Christmas cards come from twenty-three countries; you think Fruit Loops are the latest cereal rage; and the kids down the street say, "Hey, have you ever gotten tall!"   MALAYSIA

Missionaries all face the problem of learning a new language in the field. Our son David, eight, commented one day, "I sure wish they hadn't built that Tower of Babel."

✗ ○ ✗

I like Cheerios and ice cream bars and my mom's brownies, but who ever would bring prunes to a church pancake breakfast. They're so wrinkled; who would ever eat them!   BONNIE, 5

✗ ○ ✗

When my daddy prays if we'll be going to a mission place in Africa, it seems like God has only three answers: maybe, someday, not yet.

ADAM, 6

✗ ○ ✗

My mommy is excited about going to America, because there you don't even have to cook—just open a can or a box!   DANIELLE, 8

✗ ○ ✗

At our church's potluck supper, my sister said, "Oh, look—all down your pretty blouse, you've got lasagna-on-ya!"

At Sunday school, the topic of the day was how God blesses us with the seasons of the year. "Does anyone know the four seasons?" Our son Colton, four, said, "Yes, ma'am—deer season, turkey season, squirrel season, and Christmas season."

✗ ○ ✗

Pretending he was a circus announcer at our Sunday school picnic, our two-year-old grandson, Braedon, stood on a stool and shouted, "Ladies and gentlemen and gentlechildren."

✗ ○ ✗

I know our church bus driver's favorite color. It's red, 'cause every time a traffic light is red, she just stops and looks at it.   HOLLY, 5

✗ ○ ✗

One evening at church, Chad, five, was with us in the pew. We had come to hear the Christmas cantata. While there had been some quiet visiting with neighbors throughout the sanctuary, as the choir came in, everyone hushed and was attentive to their arrival. As they stood in the choir loft facing the congregation, there was a pause to await word from the preacher. All of a sudden, with a puzzled expression on his face, Chad said too loudly to his mother, "I don't hear any music, do you?"

By the time our son Billy was nine, he had had eighteen different homes, as I traveled with my family from city to city setting up Billy Graham Crusades. At dinner one evening, he said, "Dad, when will we settle down? I wish we could live on a pig farm or something like that." I tried to spiritually explain how the Lord had led me in this work and the whole family was a part of it. Almost as if he were embarrassed that he had asked, he snapped back, "But, Dad, I'm only nine years old and do you realize I've been in the ministry all my life?"

BILL BROWN,
former Billy Graham Crusade Director,
and retired president of World Wide Pictures

✗ ○ ✗

Families with small children have various phrases for "using the toilet." One of the more commonly used ones is "going potty." One day my four-year-old daughter and I were visiting in the home of a Japanese friend who had a moderate grasp on the English language. Our daughter suddenly realized it was time for her to use the rest room, and she announced publicly, "I gotta go potty." My friend looked puzzled and thoughtful. A few minutes later she ventured the question she had been pondering, "Why is it that Americans think going to the rest room is like 'going to a party?'" Japanese pronounce the word "party" as "pah-ty," just like my daughter had done a few minutes before. Oh, the joys of cross-cultural communication!

JAPAN

In our kids' church service yesterday, the guy in charge said, "God comes through a private door into every kid's heart." Isn't that neat? GLORIA, 9

✗ ○ ✗

My four-year-old sister was caught finger-painting the wall in the Sunday school girls' room. Next thing you know, she'll be spray-painting my mom's new Honda! CAROL, 7

✗ ○ ✗

Here in a land of few white people, I was buying fresh bread in a corner shop with our son Micah. He asked, "Mom, are we 'toubabs' " (local word for white people) "Actually, yes, we are," I answered. Without skipping a beat, Micah said, "That's OK. I'm not afraid, 'cause God is with us."

WEST AFRICA

✗ ○ ✗

Joshua, a seventh-grader at a Christian school that has existed for over one hundred years, often heard the alumni fret over the changes that have taken place in recent years. One day, when his Bible teacher came to class dressed like Moses, Josh turned to a classmate and said, "I don't know what this school's coming to. Now we even have a Bible teacher who's a cross-dresser!"

The trustees issued special receipts to the kids in our Sunday school who gave a dollar from their allowances toward our church's building fund: "Sanctuary Much."

✗ ⊘ ✗

It's weird; some kids just don't get the message: At Sunday school, you're supposed to put a dime or a quarter in the money basket. Some don't. I know the Bible says we mustn't gossip. Is it gossip if I tell the teacher about those other kids who don't?   RACHAEL, 7

✗ ⊘ ✗

Discussing the annual Sunday school picnic, our teacher was asking for suggestions for food and refreshment. "Nothin', except M&Ms, pizza, an' I'm bringing my Game Boy."

✗ ⊘ ✗

Sarah's first-grade Sunday school teacher gave her a compliment about her birthday dress. Sarah said, "Yes, I like it, too, but my mom says it's one big pain in the neck to iron!"

✗ ⊘ ✗

How do you like my pink pants? I just dyed them in red ink.   RONNIE, 10

Home from Sunday school, our daughter Carol, four, said, "Mama, today the teacher said God made all human 'beans.' " I said, "No, human beings, dear." Carol replied, "What's those?"

✗ O ✗

Driving home from the morning worship service, Amanda, nine, said, "Two things I liked best about that church: the children's sermon time and that closing prayer time."

✗ O ✗

When a missionary friend mentioned she was taking some Japanese girls to visit Toronto, young Katherine said, "Mommy, they're going to see the Lone Ranger's friend!"

✗ O ✗

Just think, in twelve years I'll graduate. Then I'll get married, but first I'll have to find a boyfriend. That shouldn't be so hard.   SHAREN, 6

✗ O ✗

I was just wondering what came first—Jesus or cowboys?

MARK, 7

Man, at the end of the day, those guys really have me worn out—the Devil trying to catch me, and the Lord trying to hold onto me!   DAVID, 9

✗ ◯ ✗

We asked Tom, seven, why he'd been such a bad boy lately. He answered, "I guess, like, I've had my lights on dim."

✗ ◯ ✗

One of our little missionary kids looked out the window one Saturday morning; the weather was terrible. With some disgust, he said, "Lord, you can't do this to me!"

✗ ◯ ✗

Otie, age six, had a question and an answer: "What do you call a girl pig? I guess it must be a hoggess."

✗ ◯ ✗

I have a compliment for the cook," said a missionary's kid: "Why do we have so much rice?" "Because rice is good for you. . .but what's the compliment?" "Oh, my fault. I always get compliment mixed up with complaint!"

I like everything about school, except school!

MARDI, 9

✗ ○ ✗

Is it better to twiddle your thumbs backward or forward?

ALLEN, 6

✗ ○ ✗

I got a spanking, but it didn't hurt at all, and I didn't cry; it was so light, it felt like a feather—well, almost!

DEDE, 7

✗ ○ ✗

Several years ago, five-year-old Missy attended church with a friend. When she got home, she picked up her new teddy bear and said, "I'm going to name him Gladly," she said, "because at church today they sang, 'Gladly the Cross-Eyed Bear.' "

✗ ○ ✗

Traveling to a church convention on a Sunday afternoon, a missionary-speaker noticed he'd failed to polish his shoes. So he stopped at the airport shoeshine chair. He asked the young entrepreneur if he'd been to church that morning. The young man said, "Nope, I get my church off the radio."

One morning, I told the three-year-olds in my Sunday school class the story of Mary and Joseph traveling by donkey to Bethlehem. For a snack I made sugar cookies cut with a donkey-shaped cookie cutter and I'd dipped them in cinnamon and sugar so the donkey would look fuzzy. One little boy said, "Oh, boy! It's got cin-mon on it. I love cin-mon." The little girl next to him rolled her eyes. "Not cin-mon," she said. "It's cim ma ma mom!"

✗ ⊘ ✗

I asked my three-year-old daughter, Rochelle, what her Sunday school Bible story was about. She replied, "A fat man named Josh." The Sunday school teacher told me later that is was actually Jehoshaphat, not "Josh is fat."

✗ ⊘ ✗

Driving home from our church's monthly Communion service, our four-year-old son, Tom, said, "OK, you guys had a snack at church; now, can we stop at McDonald's for me?"

✗ ⊘ ✗

Kim was five years old; he was all dressed up in a new suit and tie for the Sunday service. Our pastor said, "We'll now take up your tithes and offerings." Kim turned to me and said, "Do I have to put in my new tie?"

I was teaching a class of girls in first-grade Sunday school. Every Sunday, we took up the offering. One day, one of the girls heard someone tell me they liked my new dress. The next Sunday the superintendent came into our class because we were having a special offering. She asked the girls if they knew where their offerings were going, and one little girl piped up right away and said, "Yes, that's so Miss Edith can buy a new dress and always look nice."

✗ ○ ✗

Home from a youth crusade, our teen daughter said, "The kids' choir was neat. And their last song they did acapulco."

✗ ○ ✗

Following nine-year-old Jonathan's baptism, he whispered to his dad, "I'm so happy that my smile is almost jumping off my face!"

✗ ○ ✗

I asked this missionary who spoke at our church if he could use my dad in the Congo. He asked, "What does he do?" I said he's a used-car dealer. For a moment, the guy from the Congo was thoughtful. Then he said, "If your dad loves the Lord, you bet we can use him!"   LEONARD, 9

Shortly after returning from furlough in the United States, I overheard our five-year-old son, Jared, tell someone that he had lost twenty-five pounds since coming back to Japan. I was puzzled, wondering why our son would tell such an obvious untruth, until I saw him weighing himself again a few days later. It dawned on me that I'd forgotten to explain to him the difference between American pounds and Japanese kilograms. He was fifty pounds on the American scale, but about twenty-five kilograms on the Japanese scale. Time for a lesson in metrics!   JAPAN

TWISTED WORDS

"Mom! Come quick! God's put biscuits all over your tree!"
Darrell, age four, said, after seeing our young white hibiscus tree bloom
for the first time.

Lisa, five, was explaining to her sister Joy, two,
that Tim wanted to marry Aunt Serena,
and he gave her a ring.
"And now she's in a cage." (engaged)

After a behavior discussion on the way home from church,
our Karen said to her younger brother,
"You heard what Mommy said. She doesn't like your beatitude."

When sewing paper circles in my pre-K class,
I said to the children, "We are really sewing."
One little one looked up and said,
"No, we are really needling!"

With a marker in her hand,
Briana told her first-grade teacher,
"This pen ran out of batteries."

Meghan started kindergarten this past September.
She came home so excited and told her mother that she had learned
the Pledge of Allegiance. "I pledge allegiance to the flag
of the United States of America and to the public where the midget stands."

WHAT KIDS SAY ABOUT LIFE, LOVE, AND GOD—113

So Jesus grew
both in height and in wisdom,
and he was loved by God
and by all who knew him.

LUKE 2:52

7

Wisdom

X O X

If God really cares about a little sparrow,
isn't it super He cares about a big girl like me?

SANDY, 6

Those who know children realize that children have wisdom to impart to adults. Children put their own spin on everyday occurrences and give adults new ways of looking at life. Sometimes it is the simple joy or beauty that adults take for granted; sometimes their youthful interpretation of sayings or events causes adults to see things in a different light; often, it is children's cut-and-dried, commonsense approach to matters that makes adults wonder at their insight.

True wisdom comes from revering the Lord and obeying His commands. The world's idea of wisdom does not match God's Word. Proverbs 11:2 (NIV) says, "with humility comes wisdom," and children are certainly examples of humility. If we listen to children, we discover a new meaning for the words *wisdom* and *truth*. As we take time to teach and guide children, their wisdom and understanding will grow in depth and in scope.

While I visited the home of an African-American member of my church committee, our sons, both five years old, played together. Driving home, my son said, "Mother, that's the first time I've ever played with a boy named George."

✗ ○ ✗

One of Amy's favorite songs at age three was, "Oh, Be Careful, Little Eyes, What You See." After going through the several verses, "Be careful, little hands, what you do. . .little ears what you hear. . .little feet where you go," she added one of her own: "Oh, be careful, little nose, what you knows."

✗ ○ ✗

Three-year-old Justus and his mom were in the car on a very rainy day. The windshield wipers were going at a furious rate. After watching them for a while, Justus said, "Don't they remind you of Easton and me arguing and wrestling, back and forth, back and forth!"

✗ ○ ✗

Our three-year-old, Tory, was excitedly trying to describe a recent storm. He told how the thunder boomed; then after several unsuccessful attempts at explaining the lightning, he exclaimed, "The sky just broke all over!"

My granddaughter Lori and I were discussing hair coloring. I said, "I don't have too much gray." She replied, "Have you looked in the mirror lately?"

✗ ○ ✗

When Shane, five, was told that he used his imagination a lot, he asked, "Can I use up all my imagination?"

✗ ○ ✗

Stephanie, two, and her mother admired the beautiful sunset with its many colors. Later, when the sun had disappeared and the sky was dark, Stephanie asked, "Mommy, where did the sky go?"

✗ ○ ✗

While departing Orlando Airport, our plane was in a long line of departures inching along the runway, awaiting its turn to take off. Our youngest son, Mark, watching out the window, caught sight of a Boeing 727 just as it rotated on its takeoff roll. "Look, Dad, the pilot popped a wheelie."

✗ ○ ✗

Justus, five, is very much into words. As he bit into his Burger King hamburger, he said, "Isn't the texture of this dinner just wonderful?"

Four-year-old Stephen had only seen tomatoes in cans. But when he visited a farm, he saw them growing on a vine. He asked, "Are those tomatoes? Oh! What a good idea!"

✗ O ✗

While I was sitting on the couch sewing, I noticed four-year-old Terry crawling around at my feet. "What are you doing down there?" I asked. He looked up and said, "Mum, I heard you say you'd dropped a stitch, so I'm trying to find it." SCOTLAND

✗ O ✗

The Vermont autumn leaves were in full splendor when a small voice from the backseat of our car said, "We have an evergreen tree in our yard. I feel sorry for it because it will never be as beautiful as these other trees."

NICOLE, 6

✗ O ✗

Eight-year-old Ellen was telling her friend, "If your mom says you can't have a TV in your room, don't go over her head to God. Kids everywhere are bugging Him for stuff their moms and dads say 'no' to. So He'll just say no, too. Forget it. Just go watch the TV on the sunporch."

When Christy was four, she learned her first and last name, phone number, and address. One day I asked her, "Where do you live?" She responded, "Right here!"

✗ ο ✗

The Ten Commandments, what's that?" asked our youngest. His seven-year-old brother answered, "Oh, that's God's stop sign!"

✗ ο ✗

When my grandson Kim, age nine, was showing signs of spiritual growth, he said, "My sister Helen drives me nuts. I keep telling myself, no matter what, God is in control of everything—even Helen!"

✗ ο ✗

On a clear July night in the Austrian Alps, our nine-year-old daughter and I saw a falling star. She said, "That's God—striking a match across the sky."

✗ ο ✗

I asked our grandson, six, if he'd made up his Santa list yet. He said, "No. God knows what I want. And He'll tell Santa."

You can't see your eyes unless you look in the mirror.   Tony, 5

✗ ○ ✗

Hearing her dad complain about the high cost of long-distance phone calls, Sarah, age seven, said, "A call to God is free!"

✗ ○ ✗

One day, six-year-old Christy made this comment about the authors of her schoolbooks that have questions at the end of each chapter: "These guys don't know very much. They have to ask all the questions."

✗ ○ ✗

Five-year-old Bill's grandmother was fixing a chicken. He asked her, "Grandma, why do you call it dressing a chicken when you are undressing it?"

✗ ○ ✗

Gary worked for the security system at the Staples store. He said to his son Shawn, "See, that little emblem on the door says 'Wells Fargo.'" Shawn said, "But, Dad, how does that little sticker keep out the bad guys?"

Nine-year-old Al was severely rebuked for picking on his older sister. So he said, "Daddy was telling me about this old Christian Dutch lady named Corrie someone. . .and she said God told her if she threw all the bad stuff she did in the lake, it would, like, sink to the bottom, and He would, like, forget it. So she could, like, make, sort of a U-turn in her life—from bad stuff to good stuff. And, Mom, that's like me—now."

✗ ○ ✗

Lucy, five, was watching a sad film on television, trying hard not to cry. When her big sister noticed, Lucy claimed, "I'm not crying; my eyes are just sweating."

✗ ○ ✗

During his bedtime prayer on the first night of our vacation, our Greg, eight, said, "God, Daddy really got mad when we got a flat tire coming here. I won't tell You his name, but please be nice to all daddies who got mad today."

✗ ○ ✗

Chelsea was seven when she asked, "Mom, is corn a vegetable or animal?" "It's a vegetable," I said. Chelsea replied, "Then how come it's got a bone in the middle?"

Little Sandi sat on Santa's lap. "Would you like a nice Barbie doll?" Santa asked. In disgust, Sandi said in a loud voice, "Don't you remember, Santa, you brought me one of those last year?"

✗ ⭕ ✗

I am going to call George Washington. I found his phone number on the dollar bill.
JESSICA, 5

✗ ⭕ ✗

We adopted an African boy who was born without his lower arms or legs. Zachary is a darling, happy child, a joy for all of us. During a routine doctor's visit one day, we were waiting in the reception room with another mother and her blond, blue-eyed son. This little boy came over and looked and looked at Zachary. Turning to his mother, he said, "He's different! He's really different!" I then said, "Yes, Zachary is a different color than you are, and he doesn't have the same arms and legs you do, but he's just a little boy like you are." At that, the child again said, "But he's really, really different! He's got curly hair!"
PATTY ANGLIN, *author of* Acres of Hope

✗ ⭕ ✗

When he doesn't feel good, six-year-old Herb feels better when he looks in the mirror and smiles.

One day, our preschool boys brought me a small, plastic toy horse. Daniel said, "We should throw this away because it won't stand up by itself." David quickly responded, "No, because sometimes we can play dead horse!"

✗ ⦿ ✗

My daughter Julie, six, said this about quiet people: "Their loudness is so tiny!"

✗ ⦿ ✗

Dad, I was trying to play cricket today in the park with some bigger kids, and one of them yelled at me, "Why don't you just go grow up?" I get the "go" part, but how do I grow up?   NIGEL, 6 (ENGLAND)

✗ ⦿ ✗

Without asking me, my friend took my bike from the rack at school and rode it around and did a flat tire to it. What a creep. I told her I was mad. She said she was sorry; her daddy would fix it—which he did. So my being mad turned into forgiveness. Anyway, I felt good.   SUSAN, 9

✗ ⦿ ✗

At the lake alone with her grandparents, four-year-old Beth said, "You notice your hurts more when you're lonely."

Sarah Grace was born in December. We had many discussions with our other four children regarding her name prior to her arrival. Sometime in January, Jonathan, eight, Elizabeth, seven, and Daniel, four, were discussing her name. "God named Sarah," said Daniel. "No, He did not!" replied Jonathan and Elizabeth. "Mom and Dad did!" "No," Daniel said firmly, "God named Sarah. God thought of Sarah's name, and He just put it in Mom and Dad's heads."

✗ ⊘ ✗

Sleep is where you cross over to the next day. NATHAN, 6

✗ ⊘ ✗

I've never forgotten what my Sunday school teacher told us when I was six or seven: "What you are is God's gift to you; what you make of yourself is your gift to God." HANK, 10

✗ ⊘ ✗

Two-year-old Chris was excited about Christmas. As his mother took out the decorations, she showed him his red Christmas stocking. She held it up and said, "What is Santa Claus going to put in there?" Chris answered, "His foot!"

Grandma, why are sermons so long and movies so short? LENNIE, 7

✗ O ✗

Andy, seven, was leaving for school, carrying his ski equipment. Grandma said, "I hope this snowstorm won't cancel your ski trip tonight." Andy answered very seriously, "Grandma, that's what the snow is for!"

✗ O ✗

Ian presented his latest crayon drawing to Grandma. "Lovely," she said. "Now you should sign it like all artists do." With a flourish, the five-year-old scrawled "IAN" across the entire picture, with fancy swirls. "I wrote that in poetry," he told his grandma.

✗ O ✗

While dressing for Sunday school, our son John, four, said, "If I can put whichever sock I want on any foot I want, why can't I do the same with my shoes?"

✗ O ✗

Butter comes from butterflies. RYAN, 3

My grandson Jordan is thirteen years old. When he was leaving for a few days, his sister and I told him it would be awful quiet without him. He replied, "Oh, no, I am making a tape of my voice so you won't miss it."

✗ O ✗

Our grandson David was still a preschooler when his mother found that he knew a bit of arithmetic—he added up the number of people who would be at their house for dinner. So she began asking him addition questions. One was, "How old will your older brother be when you are ten years old?" David was still having problems pronouncing sounds such as "th," "i," and "r." So he replied, "Fufteen; but it's duh second fuhteen!" "What do you mean?" Lois asked. "Well, eight, nine, ten, eleven, twelve, fufteen, fuhteen, fifteen!"

✗ O ✗

I guess this is sort of a confession: After church once, I went to the pastor's office to get a weekly schedule. Right there on a side table was a stack of offering plates, each overflowing with money—one-dollar bills, ten dollars. Bills, just sitting there. I walked over to that table, under temptation—bigtime! Then, it's true; it was like inside me I heard this whisper: "Thou shalt not steal." That was when I was eight, and sometimes I think about that pile of money and my twitching fingers. Looking back, I guess that was a victory experience!   BRIAN, 10

My four-year-old cousin was eating too many green apples off the tree in the backyard. His mother told him, "If you keep eating those green apples, you are going to get indigestion!" He went out to play, and after a while came in looking a bit green himself! "Mom," he said slowly, "I believe I've got the Reader's Digestion!"

✗ ○ ✗

A harried mother was driving her nine-year-old daughter to school one morning, a little late. She made it through a stoplight just as it turned red, and her daughter remarked, "You shouldn't have done that." Her mother replied, "Oh, Dina, you are so law-abiding!" Dina asked, "Why do people always want to bite the law, Mom?"

✗ ○ ✗

When our son Melvin was three he said, "Carry me." I said, "You can walk. Why do you think God gave you those two nice feet?" He answered, "To put nice shoes on."

✗ ○ ✗

Mom," said our six-year-old daughter Sandy, "if God really cares about a little sparrow, isn't it super He cares about a big girl like me?"

During a recent family discussion about finances, a question was raised whether or not we could afford to continue to send our son to a Christian school. He piped up, "I hope you can, because I don't want to go to a school that doesn't have God in it."

XOX

Returning home from a vacation at the seashore, we found our home had been broken into and ransacked. I was distraught at this until little Sara said, "Don't cry, Mommy, I'll pick it up."

XOX

I took our eight-year-old granddaughter, Jenny, to a community theater to see her mom perform in the cast of an ancient Greek play. The ladies in flowing robes were on the stage doing a song-and-dance number. After observing it all very closely, Jenny said, too loudly, "Nanny, is this disgusting?"

XOX

In our area, it was not unusual for us to come upon deer standing by the roadside. One night when she saw the deer transfixed by our car's headlights, our granddaughter Heather said, "Oh, look. The deer—they have Christmas lights in their eyes!"

While spending some weeks at my parents' Florida beach home, our five-year-old, Laura, expressed concern about hurricanes. "Maybe they'll have a sign: 'No hurricanes allowed here.'"

✗ ⦿ ✗

Mom," said my three-year-old son while holding up his right hand, "if this is my right hand, then is my other one the wrong hand?" NEW ZEALAND

✗ ⦿ ✗

When his grandma said she was having trouble sleeping, Andrew, eight, said, "Just close your eyes and think nice thoughts."

TWISTED WORDS

"It was neat," said our grandson Jeff
about the science lesson.
"We read the earth is round with a creator
going all around its middle."

As your words are taught,
they give light;
even the simple can understand them.

PSALM 119:130

8
The Bible

X O X

God's Word is a lamp unto children's feet.

Many children know there is something special about the Bible. Its stories hold their attention. Who wouldn't be enthralled by stories about floods and fires, kings and queens, giants and wild animals, courageous battles, and astounding miracles? These stories remain in a youngster's heart for life.

When children's behavior is guided by God's Word, there can be no argument about what is right and wrong. God knows what's best. Children are sensitive when others are wronged and are quick to point out when someone has not followed the Bible's teachings. They soon learn that we all are in need of God's mercy and salvation as outlined in His Word.

What better gift could there be for children than the knowledge and teaching of the Bible? All other gifts will eventually be outgrown, discarded, or become obsolete. But the truths from the Bible are valuable no matter where one goes in life.

David, age five, said, "Dad, if I had been in the Garden of Eden, I wouldn't have eaten that apple." Daniel, age four, joined in, "Not me, either; I couldn't reach it!"

X O X

At baseball camp, this guy is telling me it's not cool to read the Bible. I said, "Hey, man, it's a lot cooler than that warm Sprite you're drinking out here in the sun, and a lot better for you!"

JEFF, 9

X O X

Walking through the airport terminal, four-year-old Steve stopped us dead in our tracks, held up one of his fingers, and exclaimed, "Hold it, hold it; I think I see Moses." Transfixed, we noticed at a nearby telephone a man with a long, gray beard!

X O X

Man, we've got too many rules in our house; every day, another rule. Yesterday, my dad brought home a chart with ten new rules. He said they're God's rules—so important he put them in a picture frame and hung it in our front hall.

RONNIE, 7

Ashley was three and memorizing a Bible verse: "First Peter 5:7: 'Cast all your cares upon Him, for He cares for Peter Wabbit.'"

✗ ⊘ ✗

In the Bible," our son Ted, nine, asked my husband, "where does it say 'better late than still later?'" ENGLAND

✗ ⊘ ✗

During family Bible study, our seven-year-old son said, "Hey, Mom, did you know the general direction of Mt. Sinai is straight up?"

✗ ⊘ ✗

When Jesse was almost four years old, he had already developed the habit of responding to all of my calls by saying, "Yeah, Mom, in a minute." Then he'd stay put and give the same response the very next time I called. In an attempt to inspire him to a greater level of obedience, I read to him the story of Samuel, who heard the voice of God. I embellished the story with convincing theatrics and ended the Bible story by suggesting he pray to be like little Samuel. He obliged and prayed with the same emotion with which I told the story. Then he prayed, "And Lord, when you call 'Jesse, Jesse!' I'll be quick to say, 'Yes, Lord, I'll be there in a minute!'"

So Jesus rose from the dead. OK, God did that. But how in the world did Jesus ever get that huge boulder-rock away from the tomb door? C'mon, that's my question.   JENNY, 5

✗ O ✗

The Bible says nobody should ever do sins and that's exactly what I tell my brother when he puts his gum under the living room sofa.   TIM, 6

✗ O ✗

I was trying to extract my first-grader from his bed to get ready for church when he said, "Hey, wait a minute; the Bible says Sunday's supposed to be a day of rest."

✗ O ✗

OK, comic books are fun to read, but my grandma gave me a kid's Bible. I like it better than Mickey Mouse, 'cause it's filled with neat, good stuff.
                                                                    LORRAINE, 7

✗ O ✗

Sometimes, I get so mixed up on stuff," said our son Dan. "Is it the Battle of Jericho or the Battle of Geritol?"

Our twin daughters, age five, were having a heated argument when one asked, "Mommy, where in the Bible is the place where it tells Nancy how to shut up?"

✗ O ✗

Grandma," said nine-year-old Jason, "my Sunday school teacher said, like, the Bible is God's Constitution. For next week we should find the Ten Amendments; she said to ask you where they are."

✗ O ✗

After our daughter Carol, four, had heard the Scripture in Luke 17:34 (NIV) she said she wanted to sleep alone because it says "two people will be in one bed, one will be taken and the other left."

✗ O ✗

At school, my teacher said Thomas Edison invented the light bulb. Wrong. The Bible says God made the light, and the dark.　　　　　ANNIE, 6

✗ O ✗

Every single time my sister Denise is a pain in the neck, I think about one of those Ten Commandments; it says: "Thou shalt not kill."　　　DAVID, 7

A little boy was asked what he learned in Sunday school. He answered, "God must like roast beef a lot, because He owns the cattle on a thousand hills."

✗ O ✗

Oh, yes, I spend lots and lots of time going through the pages of my Bible. you see, my grandma always hides dollar bills in there for me.   Lou, 7

✗ O ✗

Our daughter Nan angrily exclaimed, "If the Holy Word didn't say we should love one another, I would pinch my sister."

✗ O ✗

One Sunday morning, my nephew, who was about four years old, asked me for a Bible. I pointed out that he could not read, he persisted, so I got him one. The next Sunday morning I was standing outside church when around the corner came my nephew. No marine ever walked so ramrod straight. Shoulders thrown back, Bible held fast by his side, Michael marched into church, looking neither right nor left. He was so proud! Though he was too young to really know the significance of owning a Bible, the "power" of the Word was evident!

Jonathan, age seven, declared, "If God created the world in six days, Adam and Eve never saw any stars." His Grandpa asked, "Why do you think that?" Jonathan's reply: "Because it takes starlight millions of years to reach the earth!"

✗ ⭕ ✗

Yes, I think there's a Bible verse that says "treat others the same way they like to treat you." That means if Melissa kicks me, I kick her back—to learn her a lesson.   JOSEPH, 4

TWISTED WORDS

Answering the phone, our four year old said, "It's for you, Papa."
I said, "Well, please bring it to me."
She replied, "I can't. It's the cordable one."

Five-year-old Rick's report on his Sunday school lesson:
"We learned all about the twelve opossums."

"Anyone who welcomes
a little child like this
on my behalf welcomes me,
and anyone who welcomes me
welcomes my Father who sent me."

MARK 9:37

9
Prayer

Χ Ο Χ

God loves me, and He will hear me.

ANTHONY, 4

Throughout the Bible, people communicate with God. Noah, Abraham, Moses, Hannah, and many others spoke intimately with God about the plans for their lives. God wants us to be in contact with Him and share our concerns and joys.

Boys and girls enjoy talking with those they love and trust, but adults often simply do not listen to children. So when children realize that God is never too busy to listen to them, imagine their excitement! They can talk to the Creator of the universe about whatever comes into their active, inquisitive minds!

Some youngsters view God as a granter of wishes with the ability to fix any problem. To others, God is a best friend or a caregiver who takes away hurts and fears. One thing is certain: God is real and hears, cares, and responds to any prayer.

Children may take turns saying grace before their meals. But their gratitude doesn't stop with food! Children are eager to thank God for all He has given them—from toys, to pets, to nature, to homes and families, to His love and salvation. How the Lord must enjoy hearing these young ones praise Him!

When our grandson was three years old, we sat down to eat lunch. I told him we would pray silently this time. So he bowed his head and said, "Silently, silently, silently."

✗ ○ ✗

Here is the bedtime prayer of three-year-old Stephanie: "Help my cold to get better, help Mommy's cold to get better, and help Daddy's cold to get better. And, Jesus, don't You get a cold!"

✗ ○ ✗

Our four-year-old daughter was sitting on my lap while I was mowing our lawn with a power mower. When we came up to a tree, the gear wouldn't reverse. She said, "Let's pray and ask Jesus to help us get unstuck." We did. The mower still didn't reverse. She then said, "Don't worry. He's busy now. Just wait. He will help."

✗ ○ ✗

My grandson had already started eating his lunch before his daddy came to the table. When Daddy started eating, his son reminded him that he needed to ask a blessing. His daddy said, "I just prayed to myself." The son said, "Well, I pray mine to God!"

It was the first day at day care for our great-grandson Anthony, age four. His mother came to have lunch with him, and Anthony bowed his head to say his blessing. Another little boy said, "Why are you doing that? It's dumb." Anthony looked at his mother with a tear in his eye. He turned to the other boy and said, "God loves me, and He will hear me."

✗ ⦿ ✗

Our three-year-old son, Bill, heard me say I had a headache. To my surprise, that night in prayer he prayed, "Pleeeze, God, give Mama a new head." I didn't get a new head, but I surely received a warm heart!

✗ ⦿ ✗

One evening, just as we sat down to dinner, bowing our heads for the blessing, the phone rang. Eight-year-old Jeremy answered it, saying, "Dear Jesus—I mean, hello?"

✗ ⦿ ✗

Seven-year-old DeAndra likes whole raw milk, fresh from the cow. She does not like milk from the store. So she prayed last night, "Father in heaven, thank You for this food, and especially for this milk—this good raw milk we get here at Grandma's house."

At two years old, Jeremy didn't forget his sisters in his bedtime prayer: "I love Amy down to sleep, I pray to Lori my soul to keep."

✗ ○ ✗

I told our granddaughter Katherine, five, that God answers our prayers by sometimes saying "no," sometimes "yes," and sometimes "wait." She thought about this a minute and then said, "But why doesn't He take away my freckles?"

✗ ○ ✗

And from the Lord's Prayer: "Give us this day our jelly bread, and lead us not into Penn Station." JENNIE, 4

✗ ○ ✗

After arriving in Bombay, I was hospitalized with chronic headaches. The doctor scheduled a spinal tap. Our son Douglas, eleven, prayed: "Dear Lord, help the doctor so that when he examines Daddy's head, he'll find nothing in it." INDIA

✗ ○ ✗

Please, God, don't make us behave better; me and Curt are having lots of fun just the way we are. SEAN, 6

A kitten belonging to a Romanian pastor became stranded in a tree. To get it down, the pastor threw a rope over the branch and tied it to his car's bumper. Driving slowly forward, he pulled the branch down to within reach. Just then the rope snapped, and the frightened feline went flying up in the air and was nowhere to be found.

The next day the pastor met a neighbor. "You'll never believe what happened yesterday!" she exclaimed. "My little girl had been begging for a kitten, but I told her she could have one only if Jesus gave it to her. So she ran outside, knelt down, and prayed, 'Jesus, please give me a kitty of my very own to love and care for. Amen.' Just then a kitten with paws out-stretched fell right out of heaven!"

Whether or not this story is true, it makes the point that asking is basic to prayer. Jesus taught His disciples to say, "Give us," "Forgive us," "Deliver us" (Matthew 6:11–13). But our asking must always be based on a desire to please God and to advance His purposes on earth (Matthew 6:9–10, 33). James said, "You ask and do not receive, because you ask amiss, that you may spend it on your pleasures" (James 4:3 NKJV). That's why we must learn about God from His Word. Then our asking will glorify Him.

DENNIS J. DE HAAN

✗ ○ ✗

Our grandson, eight, asked if he could say grace after our Sunday dinner. "Of course," I said. "OK, God, that chicken stuff was really neat, but why did You ever invent tapioca pudding? Amen."

My little grandnephew gave me a creative definition of faith and works. He and his smaller brother went to the nursery at church each Sunday. A bully there bothered them. After church one Sunday, I asked the two little fellows, "How did it go today?" The older of the two said, "Oh, fine! This big guy tried to push us around, so I prayed to the Lord and I punched him in the stomach, and then he leaved us alone."

✗ ⊘ ✗

Time for going-to-sleep prayers," I said to five-year-old Helen. "Yes, Mom." "But I can't hear you," I said. "No," was the answer, " 'cause I'm, like, praying in my head."

✗ ⊘ ✗

Now this friend of mine, he never says his prayers. I tell him I like to pray. He says stuff like, "Oh, that's just feel-good selfishness." Last time he said that, I said, "You've got a feel-bad problem!"   CYNTHIA, 9

✗ ⊘ ✗

I wish my Grandpa Pat didn't die, and I pray God will give the poor people lots of food.   MELANIE, 7

I said to our daughter Abigail: "Don't forget to pray for a house for us to live in when we move to Florida, so we won't have to live in a box." "Dear Jesus," she prayed, "please help Daddy find a house for us to live in in Florida." Then she looked at me and said, "There, now we won't have to live in a box."

✗ O ✗

Our eight-year-old grandson's graces could go into a book. A recent example: "Lord, Grandma needs a new iced-tea pitcher and, while You're at it, how about a new pitcher for our Little League team?"

✗ O ✗

A seven-year-old's prayer: "God, those bad people laughed at Noah—building that ark and all on the mountain. But Noah stuck with You. Me, too. Amen."

✗ O ✗

Our son, five, prayed: "Now I lay me down. . .God, while You're listening, make Jeff happy and Don happy and Uncle Glen happy, and You please be happy, too."

When my granddaughter Teri was six, we asked her to say grace at the table. Teri sat quietly with her hands folded and head bowed and then whispered, "Grace."

✗ ⊘ ✗

Six-year-old Ellen's prayer: "God, You know something? I help my brother a lot of times. If You just ask me, I'll help You answer other kids' prayers and stuff."

✗ ⊘ ✗

Pastor Bob and his wife, Betty, invited two couples from their congregation for dinner. When they sat down to eat, Pastor Bob asked his young son Bobby to say grace. Bobby was at a loss for words, so his mother whispered, "Just say what you heard me say." With head bowed, Bobby said, "Dear Lord, why did we invite people on such a hot day? Amen."

✗ ⊘ ✗

Bobby, six, went out on his front porch one day and looked up and down the street for someone to play with. Seeing no one, he cupped his hands to his mouth and shouted at the top of his lungs, "Will somebody please come out and play with me, in the name of the Lord!"

Hey, I know one thing about praying: You've got to listen—just listen to God. He's got a lot of information and advice about everything.

ROBERT, 8 (DENMARK)

✗ ◯ ✗

Four-year-old Hank asked his mother to buy him a red wagon for Christmas. So, she said, "Why not pray about it?" He did: "God, I really do want a little red wagon, but isn't tomorrow better than Christmas?"

✗ ◯ ✗

When suggesting to our grandson that we needed to pray about a problem he was having with his younger brother, his sister spoke up and explained, "Now, you can always talk to God, but if He doesn't answer right away, that means He's busy with someone else's problem, you know."

✗ ◯ ✗

Some years ago, we moved from Hollywood to Inglewood. On the first evening in our new home, our youngest son prayed, "Our Father, who art in heaven, Inglewood be Thy name." Later we asked, "Why Inglewood?" "Well, when we lived in Hollywood, we always prayed, 'Hollywood be Thy name,' didn't we?"

Our granddaughter Tammy prayed, ". . .And if I should die before I wake, I'll just call the doctor."

✗ o ✗

Soon after our family joined the world of computers, our Helen, seven, closed her bedtime prayer this way: ". . .But deliver us some E-mail."

SWITZERLAND

✗ o ✗

One day, when our town was hit by a severe thunder and lightning storm, our great-grandson said he was afraid. . .so, "Mama, let's just go into your room, close the door, and pray together."

✗ o ✗

When my husband told our son, three, it was time to say his bedtime prayers, the boy said, "No, not now, because I'm playing. So you go ahead and get started praying without me."

✗ o ✗

The four most important words in prayer are *God, yes, please,* and *thanks.*

PETER, 4

Our son Simon said grace at his sixth birthday party: "God, You and Jesus are so very old. Yet You love us little kids, and You know we like all this ice cream and cake and Cokes and presents and stuff. Thanks a million!"

✗ ○ ✗

One evening when I was praying, our four-year-old grandson, Cory, said, "Wait a minute. Stop right there!" I didn't stop—just went on praying, and then said, "Don't you ever again interrupt someone who's praying!" His response: "Well, you didn't have to pray that long, did you?"

✗ ○ ✗

I stopped praying," announced our son Steven, age five. "The deal is," he explained, "at Sunday school they said that, no matter what, God knows exactly what we're thinking. So, from now on, I'm just gonna think about stuff with my eyes closed."

Some children were brought
to Jesus so he could lay his hands
on them and pray for them.
The disciples told them
not to bother him.
But Jesus said,
"Let the children come to me.
Don't stop them!
For the Kingdom of Heaven belongs
to such as these."

MATTHEW 19:13–14

10
Heaven

X O X

Someday, Mommy, we can all be together in heaven.

JACOB, 6

Heaven must be difficult for a child to imagine. When children learn about heaven, they hear that it is a wonderful, happy, joyful place where they will be with God. But what about the details? Details are so very important to children. How will they actually get up there? Exactly what will heaven look like? How can people live in the sky? What will they do all day? These are important issues to children.

Heaven can seem a mysterious place, but thinking about it can be comforting to children. There they will see beloved grandparents and other loved ones who have died. There won't be anything scary or mean in heaven. No cuts or scrapes or sore throats or stomachaches are allowed in heaven.

All of us, to some extent, have a childlike inquisitiveness when we ponder heaven. How will it feel to be there forever? Imagine talking to Jesus, Moses, David, and Elijah and, most exciting of all, seeing God face-to-face! Jesus told His disciples when He blessed the children that the kingdom of heaven belongs to such little ones. With childlike faith and trust, we await our heavenly home.

I have lots of questions about Jesus—like up there in heaven, does He have to keep His room neat? Does He take the subway to His office, like my dad? Where does He go for vacation? How does He know the good kids from the bad ones? And, He must have a lot of assistants to hear all of our family's prayers. I mean, we pray every day, and there's six of us!   CLIFF, 5

✗ ○ ✗

Mom, God's so neat, and heaven's supposed to be so great. Could me and Gloria go there Saturday for a sleep-over?   BETSY, 6

✗ ○ ✗

Our seven-year-old daughter, Clarisa, was not really excited about going to Sunday school, but her little friend talked her into it. After the first class, at lunch she said, "I like my teacher, and she said if I come to Sunday school every Sunday, she'll show me how I can get a free trip to heaven!"

✗ ○ ✗

My three-year-old granddaughter, Morgan, came over one day and looked around the room and asked, "Where's Grandpa?" I answered, "He is in heaven." Surprised, she looked at me and said, "Still?"

I have three dogs—Trixie, Scamp and Ebony. But Ebony lives in heaven right now. CHRISTOPHER, 5

✗ O ✗

Those stars—way up there like that. God should have some bright lights in heaven, instead of those billions of dim bulbs. STUART, 6

✗ O ✗

I know what heaven is like, because I was there. God makes people when He thinks of them, and then they wait to be born. BETH, 4

✗ O ✗

Before a special Christmas worship service, the organist played "Silent Night." Our son Alex, five, commented: "Guys, don't you hear that song they're playing? I think it's that sleep-in-heaven one."

✗ O ✗

Our six-year-old, Rachel, prayed, "God, they keep telling us You love us kids. But I'm wondering: If You know my older brother, do You think he'll ever get to heaven?"

When our daughter Sarah, seven, heard her great-grandmother had died, she asked her grandmother, "Did she wear a pretty dress when she met Jesus?"

✗ ○ ✗

Grandma's gone to heaven, and she'll be happy there, because there's a Dairy Queen everywhere. Right?   LUCIA, 6

✗ ○ ✗

Getting old like Grandpa is going to be fun. And then someday, Mommy, we can all be together in heaven.   JACOB, 6

✗ ○ ✗

Heaven—as viewed through the hearts and minds of Becca, Sarah, Abigail, Heather, Michael, and Rachael—all of Newtown Square, PA.

I think heaven will be glamorous, shining, sparkling, glorious, and wonderful. When Jesus returns, I think it will be like this: a big cloud with gold, and Jesus bringing all His little children and Christians who believe in Him up to heaven. In heaven, I think there will be angels, and Daniel will be there, and Mary, Joseph, Rebekah, and Rahab. I think it will be amazing. Heaven will be the best place ever. I am so glad I will get to go to heaven. I would love to meet Jesus, and someday I will. That's why I am so happy. I hope that heaven is wonderful just like I think it will be.   BECCA, 8

I think heaven will have a pearly and golden gate so we can enter His kingdom, and then we could ask questions about stuff we really wanted to know about. And they have streets of gold. I can't wait to go there when I'm old. It sounds like a very peaceful place. SARAH, 9

X O X

I think heaven will be made with gold and will be prettier than the nicest things ever. And heaven will be perfect. You'll have everything you want. But one question I'd like to know is, if you die before the Second Coming, what age would you look like? A baby? A teenager? An adult? A senior citizen? I guess I will have to wait. But I won't mind. I like to wonder. ABIGAIL, 9

X O X

I think that heaven will be beautiful, and it'll be bright from God. Maybe the streets of gold will be so bright that we'll have to wear sunglasses. When I was little, I thought that when there was a thunderstorm the angels were bowling. And I would say, "Strike! Good one, God," because He is so powerful. And when I smelled the barbecue grill, I would say, "Mmm, God's having a feast." I think heaven will be great! HEATHER, 9

I think heaven is going to be very fun. I wonder if we will be able to fly or if we could swim in water and not get wet. That would be fun if we could walk through flowers. And be really good in math.

MICHAEL, 9

✗ O ✗

I think heaven will have streets of gold. Then I wonder, would we have gold hair when we go to heaven? I think that heaven is going to be perfect. I think that when Jesus comes, He is going to have angels at His side when He is riding in a chariot. I would love to see Jesus' face. I would ask Him questions.

RACHAEL, 8

✗ O ✗

Question-and-answer time with our son Terry (six): "What's the difference between God and Jesus?" Answer: "Nothin'. They're just like my daddy, except They live on the same street—up in heaven."

✗ O ✗

When Jenny was four, she asked, "Does heaven have a floor?" Surprised, I said, "Well, Jenny, what do you think heaven is like?" She looked up at the sky and clouds and replied, "Well, I can't see any floor, so I guess people are just up there on coat hangers!"

Mom, when you die and go to heaven, every time you hear Gabriel blow his horn, are you going to look to see if it is me coming?   JENNIE, 5

✗ o ✗

I told nine-year-old Heather that someday we would have glorified bodies. She asked, "Do you think we'll look like Barbie?"

✗ o ✗

Sunlight in several hanging prisms was causing rainbows to flash across the wall of our Sunday school classroom. Observing this, Chris, four, whose mother had recently died, said, "Know what? My mom's helping God make those rainbows!"

✗ o ✗

Our granddaughter Erica, eight, was afraid to fly, but she didn't want to stay home when we went to visit Canada. While on the flight, I said, "Look out the window at the beautiful white clouds!" She said, "Wow! It's just like being in heaven!" I suggested it might be nice if we could go to heaven. Her response: "No, first I want to go home and see my daddy!"

I was planning for our family's summer vacation with ideas from the AAA about tours of New England. Simon, age seven, said, "How 'bout asking the Triple-A about a heaven tour? It'd be fun to go there, too."

χ ο χ

My four-year-old granddaughter, Kristie, and I were out for a ride. I commented, "This is the town where your dad's grandfather lived." "Where is he now?" "He was old and died and went to heaven," I replied. "Oh, Grammy," she said, "you and I will never get old."

χ ο χ

When our beloved cocker spaniel, Cokie, was killed by a car, our little Lucie was crushed. The Lord gave me just the right words: "Honey, now Cokie will be able to run and play safely forever." Lucia regained her composure and said, "Mom, you mean like in heaven?"

χ ο χ

One day my five-year-old grandson, Brett, who frequently went fishing with his dad, told his mother, "If Grandma's going to heaven with us, God had better have a pretty big fishing rod to haul her in!"

My husband was a minister for forty-four years. When he was still with us, he and I traveled all over the United States, Canada, Mexico, and Alaska—also into many foreign countries. A few years before his death, our little grandson, Christian, asked his aunt about different people who had died and whether or not she felt they were in heaven. Then he began to name people still living and wanted to know, if they died, would they go to heaven? When he got to his grandfather, whom all the grandchildren called "Papaw," he said, "Well, I know my Papaw would go to heaven, because he loves Jesus and preaches all the time, and I know Mamaw would go because she goes everywhere Papaw goes."

TWISTED WORDS

Our two granddaughters,
Jayne, eight, and Brooke, ten, were visiting us,
and we were discussing temperaments.
I told Brooke she was a melancholy personality,
and Jayne said, "What's a melon collie?"

A cheerful heart is good medicine.

PROVERBS 17:22

A time to cry and a time to laugh.
A time to grieve and a time to dance.

ECCLESIASTES 3:4

He will yet fill your mouth with laughter
and your lips with shouts of joy.

JOB 8:21

11

On the Lighter Side

X O X

Daddy, did God make the paper clip before He invented me?

The next time you are feeling down in the dumps, watch children at play. Notice how they smile and laugh and seldom frown. Children have worries and problems, too, but their basic nature tends toward happiness. Not only are children fun to be with because of their innocent happiness, but the fresh way they view life is also amusing. Children approach problems as positive challenges to be overcome and mastered in their own creative and sometimes hilarious ways.

God created us with the gift of laughter. It is not His desire for us to become so downtrodden with cares and worries that we are unable to take time for enjoyment and fellowship with others—young and old.

Part 1

Ages two through five

Maybe next year I can reach the light switch.

Three-year-old Mark was drinking a glass of Kool-Aid and pouting because he couldn't join his brothers in big-boy games. A friend told him, "Mark, wipe that attitude off your face." Mark replied, "That's not attitude; it's Kool-Aid."

✗ ⚬ ✗

My great-granddaughter, three, was playing with her sisters when she stubbed her toe. I said, "Poor Mandy, did you stub your toe?" She tearfully replied, "Yes, all six of them."

✗ ⚬ ✗

While visiting friends, Michael, four, was warned to stay away from the cat. "The cat doesn't know you," I instructed. Later he approached the cat, looked it in the eye, and stated, "Hi, I'm Michael Winters." Then turning to me, he stated, "There, Grandma, now the cat knows me."

We were about to drive through an underwater tunnel when our little Stephanie said: "Oops, better put your windows up!"

✗ ⃝ ✗

Wow! That looks just like the Red Sea!" David said while watching an overturned cup of red fruit drink cascading off the table.

✗ ⃝ ✗

Ruthanne was anticipating her fourth birthday, because then she'd be a "big girl." The special day arrived, and she sighed, "I'm not a big girl yet; maybe next year I can reach the light switch!"

✗ ⃝ ✗

Early one morning, my daughter Michelle came to me with this complaint: "Mom, my arm feels all sparkly!"

✗ ⃝ ✗

After a vigorous wrestling session with our family's shedding cat, our four-year-old Darrell sputtered in disgust, "Boy, you should have asked God to glue your hair on better!"

Becca made a list of guests for her fourth birthday party: Mommy, Daddy, older sister, and six friends and neighbors. I asked her, "Don't you want to invite your aunt and uncle and cousins?" She responded: "Well, that's all the fingers I have; I can't count any more!"

✗ O ✗

Stephanie was crying about everything at breakfast, but soon she became distracted and stopped crying for a few minutes. Soon she asked, "Now, what was I crying about?"

✗ O ✗

Shortly after Princess Diana's death, our four-year-old son, Jason, said, "Remember Diana, the Queen of Dolphins?" I began to explain who Diana really was when Jason interrupted, "Oh, that's right, she was Diana, Princess of the Whales."

✗ O ✗

We hired a woman to stay with our children while we were away. One evening, she was running the bathwater for our four-year-old, Gary. But he decided he did not want to take a bath. "You are running up my dad's water bill," he protested.

When we were visiting friends on the coast, we went swimming at the beach. My little girl took one look at the ocean and said, "But I didn't want a swimming pool that big!"

✗ ⦿ ✗

Stephanie, three, had a bad ear infection, and so she colored her teddy bear's ear with a red crayon. Then she said, "There, I gave him an ear infection, too."

✗ ⦿ ✗

During the court proceedings for the adoption of our daughter, the very stern judge in his black robe completed the procedure without a single smile, although he did come down from the bench to congratulate us. As we departed, our three-year-old son, Brad, called back, "So long, Judge, see you again next year." The stone-faced judge was still laughing as we left the courthouse!

✗ ⦿ ✗

When driving across the country, we came to an area where some rabbits had been hit by passing cars. I showed them to my little boy and asked, "Do you know what will happen to you if you run in the street?" He answered, "Squashed like a bunny?"

When we told Ben, four, not to shout, he said, "I wasn't shouting. I was talking on my microphone."

✗ ○ ✗

One day, our son Ethan, five, said he was very bored: "Mom, I need some medicine. Maybe some boring medicine, so I won't be bored anymore."

✗ ○ ✗

My only auntie, visiting from Virginia, had brought me a lovely silver slotted serving spoon as a gift. Whispering in my ear, my three-year-old, Jimmy, said, "It's too bad it leaks!"

✗ ○ ✗

I was explaining to our son Mason that his great-grandmother is happy in heaven with God and that she's seeing Grandad, too. Mason said, "Yes, and probably she's even seeing Abraham Lincoln."

✗ ○ ✗

Paul, not quite six, was at a meal at church camp. The adult at his table said, "Paul, you shouldn't push your food onto your fork with your thumb." Paul replied, "Why not? My dad does it."

One afternoon we stopped by a farm store to get some eggs. Farmer Frey greeted us warmly and then took our four-year-old son to see the new baby calf. As my husband and I waited in the car, we expected to be questioned about the birds and the bees when Jimmy returned. At first he was very quiet. At last he said, "There's just one thing I don't understand. Daddy, where does grape juice come from?"

✗ ○ ✗

Our doubting young son left his tooth under his pillow with a note asking the Tooth Fairy to leave him a signed note in return. The Tooth Fairy complied with a little note and fifty cents. The next tooth he lost, he left another note asking for her picture!

✗ ○ ✗

The doctors informed our family that Grandmother was gravely ill and she might not survive. The family was gathered around her bed in the hospital when her young grandson blurted out, "Look out, God, here comes Grandma!"

✗ ○ ✗

At the reception following our nephew's wedding, our little girl whispered, "Uncle Tim kissed Aunt Vera—right there in the church! Is that OK?"

One of my preschool students asked me how we were going to get to heaven. I explained to him that those who love Jesus and ask Him to forgive their sins will live with Him in heaven one day. "Oh, OK," he answered, "I thought we were going to go by helicopter."

✗ ⊙ ✗

As our two-year-old daughter, Nina, experimented with little stones to see where they fit in tiny crannies of her body, she was admonished by her mother not to put them in her nose. "The stone would be hard to remove, and the doctor would have to go up your nose after it." Nina's eyes grew large. "The whole doctor?"

✗ ⊙ ✗

Our five-year-old grandson, James, has two older brothers who boss him around. So James has developed this philosophy: "At least I'm the boss of my shoes!"

✗ ⊙ ✗

Assuming she was put together like her favorite doll, when undressing one night, Danielle, three, checked her toes "to be sure the stuffing wasn't coming out."

During a severe thunderstorm, my three-year-old granddaughter, Brittany, said, "Grandma, Jesus is taking my picture 'cause I just saw the camera flash!"

✗ O ✗

Our five-year-old granddaughter was sitting next to a friend's little boy in the car. She started chattering incessantly to him, and, after enduring many minutes of her torrent of words, the little fellow put his hands over his ears and cried out, "I can't hear you anymore!"

✗ O ✗

When Rachel's two-year-old friend was at our house, she noticed our one hundred-pound dog lying in the corner. "Can I pet that dog?" she asked. "Oh, yes," I told her. Then she replied in a most matter-of-fact way, "But he might eat me."

✗ O ✗

During drawing period in our kindergarten class, Klaus, five, was working on a picture of electricity. "Nobody really knows what electricity looks like," I said. He replied, "Come back in ten minutes, and you'll be the first person to see it!"

GERMANY

We once went with an elderly aunt to a Catholic church service. On departing, our youngest daughter complimented the priest on his dress!

ENGLAND

✗ ○ ✗

One day, I served open-faced sandwiches for lunch. The next day, our daughter said, "I want another open-mouth sandwich today."

✗ ○ ✗

After a meal, I told Julie, three, to go wash her face. She said, "Nope, I just use my tongue."

✗ ○ ✗

Our four-year-old son said he wanted some Tooth Fairy money, but, "I don't want to lose my teeth to get it. I wouldn't be able to talk if I did," he said.

Part 2

Ages six through ten

Hey, Dad, I've got all the answers now!

One fall day, my two girls and I were walking along a road. We marveled at a flock of geese flying south for the winter. The next day, as we were walking down the same road, the geese were flying in the opposite direction! Ashley, age nine, said, "Hmmm. Maybe they forgot something!"

✗ O ✗

It was the first day out of school for the summer. Nine-year-old Gil grabbed his skateboard and left the house with these parting words: "Mom, gotta lotta livin' to do!"

✗ O ✗

Danielle, eight, was thrilled to receive a beautifully made zippered bag for her birthday. When she opened it and found a camera inside, she exclaimed, "What's this doing in here?"

Ten-year-old Phil was the pinnacle of confidence at breakfast after studying his year-end Bible history exam: "Hey, Dad, I've got all the answers now!"

✗ ○ ✗

The opposite of near is far; the opposite of in is out; the opposite of you don't have to blow your nose is you do have to blow your nose.

MELISSA, 6

✗ ○ ✗

Our kids were reflecting on past experiences: "No, I never rode my bike wearing Mom's high heels!" Her older brother: "OK, let's go to the videotape!"

✗ ○ ✗

While in Europe, Sandra, eight, was trying to explain to a local girl what white bread is. "Well," she said, "a white bread is a bread which is not black."

PORTUGAL

✗ ○ ✗

I asked young Stephen if he'd like a piece of fresh-baked apple pie. His answer: "Granny, what else have you got?"

Our six-year-old son, Sam, loved to ride on Mr. Moore's wagon when he spread manure in the fields. I asked him one day, "How can you stand the smell?" Sam's reply: "Oh, I don't use my nose when I'm out with Mr. Moore."

✗ o ✗

The nurse was preparing our eight-year-old daughter for minor surgery. To reassure her, she said, "Don't worry, honey, your doctor is very nice," to which our daughter responded, "I know he's very nice, but has he ever operated before?"

✗ o ✗

English actress Joan Winmill toured Great Britain with Bela Lugosi in the widely acclaimed play, *Dracula*. Later she married Billy Graham team member Bill Brown. Many years later, the Browns' son Bill, seven, was asked what kind of work his parents did. He answered rather shyly, "Dad works for Billy Graham." Then, with great enthusiasm he said, "But my mom used to work for Dracula!"

✗ o ✗

When scolded for not eating his vegetables, our son John, six, put his head on the table and moaned, "I can't eat any more. My teeth are tired."

Beth forgot what she wanted to say. "Oh, dear," she exclaimed, "the film is backward in my mind."

✗ ○ ✗

In my Sunday school class, one of the kids said, "God did a super job with us people and dogs and birds and stuff. But that giraffe sure turned out to be a bummer."

✗ ○ ✗

Our nine-year-old son, Jerry, advised his buddy: "Act bad if you want to. But if you're good an hour a day, all of those good hours will pay off big-time at Christmas."

✗ ○ ✗

Noah's wife said, "How can you go fishing? You have no bait." "What do ya mean, dear—no bait? Haven't I got two worms?"　　GEORGE, 9

✗ ○ ✗

Our first grandson said, "It's a human, physical fact, Grandpa, that if you sneeze, you must shut your eyes, or your eyeballs will fall out."

Mom, what is this stuff with the piano? My music teacher says I have to take those lessons for two more years to find out if I really do hate it!

MARILYN, 7

✗ ✗

Bob, age eight, closed his bedtime prayer with these words: ". . .And please give me a big box with a trillion dollars in it. Amen."

✗ ✗

My mommy tells me the two most important things in my life are God and vitamin C.

TERRY, 7

✗ ✗

Visiting her great-grandmother at a nursing home, Alice, six, said, "Mommy, where's that lady taking her towel rack?"

✗ ✗

Our son Peter, eight, had a great plan: "If you would give me a nice big raise in my allowance, then—and this will make the pastor happy—I could give a little to the church building program."

Now and then our family's dinner-table conversation is reduced to a things-we-shouldn't-have-done level. At one of those, eight-year-old Ted said, "During last week's potluck supper at the church, I got rid of my Brussels sprouts. Only problem was the pastor's wife saw me. No fun having to scrape those Brussels sprouts out of the dishwasher!"

✗ O ✗

Our teacher said we should keep an open mind. I told her, "Oh, no, then my brains will fall out!"   VICTOR, 6

✗ O ✗

We used to play games with our three kids (ages seven, five, and three) on long drives in the car. Once I asked them what the white dashed lines in the middle of the road looked like, and Dave, seven, piped up with, "They look like a line of belly-up squashed skunks lying in the middle of the road!"

✗ O ✗

At the bank, our six-year-old son noticed one of the tellers. "Mama, she is so pretty. If she's not married, I'll marry her." When I told him she had a wedding ring on her finger, he made a sound of disappointment and said, "Aw, shucks!"

Always, always, like when I wrap up a gift package, I put a Christmas band-aid on it, so they'll know it's from me. CAMILLA, 9

✗ O ✗

While I was driving our Michael and a friend from school, the boys were discussing whether or not there really is a Santa Claus. Our son said, "Of course, there is. My daddy and mommy could never afford all of that stuff!"

✗ O ✗

Our son was disappointed the Dinah Shore Christmas Show rerun wasn't about dinosaurs.

✗ O ✗

Our daughter, nine, learned in school that silk is made by silkworms. Soon thereafter, when observing I was wearing a silk blouse, she said, "Oh, dear, Mommy, you're wearing that bug-stuff blouse!"

✗ O ✗

While walking on a nature trail with our homeschool group, we came upon a mounted exhibit with leaf samples from area trees. Thomas, age six, pointed to one of the larger leaves. "Look, Adam's underwear!"

We had a lovely dinner party arranged to welcome our new pastor and his wife. As the guests were taking their places 'round the dinner table, I asked our ten-year-old, Hank, to pull out the pastor's wife's chair. He did, and the dear lady ended up seated on the floor!

TWISTED WORDS

Sonia, our six-year-old granddaughter,
was with us on holiday in Portugal.
She greeted the housemaid every morning with "Obnigado"
(Portuguese for hello).
On the maid's morning off, she inquired,
Where is Obnigado this morning?"

PORTUGAL

Jessica, five, came home with the news:
"My music teacher is leaving because
she is old and she is getting retarded."

In response to a discussion about
the importance of getting
the proper amount of sleep,
Stephanie, seven, said,
"I think I'm nocturnal."

Why did God make rainbows?
So Noah could learn his colors!
MEGHAN, 3

God made the clouds go 'round and round the world.
Where else?
MIKE, 7

About the Authors

After university graduation, Mary Barbour gained her first writing experience during her years with a New York advertising agency. In recent years, with her husband Bill, she co-authored two widely selling books in the field of international travel.

For forty years, Bill Barbour served with the century-old book publisher, Fleming H. Revell Company—retiring some years ago as the firm's chairman and CEO. More recently a book-writing team, during their Revell years the Barbours worked closely with Corrie ten Boom, Helen Steiner Rice, Dale Evans Rogers, Charles L. Allen, David Wilkerson, Tom Landry, and other leaders in the Christian writing community. The Barbours have three children, nine grandchildren, and reside in Ft. Myers, Florida.

For nearly twenty years, Rebekah Rendall Blanda has played an active role in working with young children and teens—in churches, Sunday schools, and schools. She majored in childhood education and Spanish at the University of Richmond, Virginia, and then taught for four years in the Richmond Public Schools. Now a writer of note, she is currently the prekindergarten teacher at an inner-city Christian school in Philadelphia, the city in which newlyweds Rebekah and John Blanda now live.